10/11

THE
TEN-MINUTE
GARDENER'S
VEGETABLE-
GROWING
DIARY

www.**transworldbooks**.co.uk

Also by Val Bourne

The Natural Garden
The Winter Garden
Seeds of Wisdom

The Ten-Minute Gardener's Flower-Growing Diary
The Ten-Minute Gardener's Fruit-Growing Diary

THE
TEN~MINUTE
GARDENER'S
VEGETABLE~
GROWING
DIARY

Val Bourne

in association with
The Daily Telegraph

BANTAM PRESS

LONDON · TORONTO · SYDNEY · AUCKLAND · JOHANNESBURG

TRANSWORLD PUBLISHERS
61–63 Uxbridge Road, London W5 5SA
A Random House Group Company
www.transworldbooks.co.uk

First published in Great Britain
in 2011 by Bantam Press
an imprint of Transworld Publishers

A CIP catalogue record for this book
is available from the British Library.

ISBN 9780593066713

Addresses for Random House Group Ltd companies outside the UK
can be found at: www.randomhouse.co.uk
The Random House Group Ltd Reg. No. 954009

The Random House Group Limited supports the Forest Stewardship Council (FSC®),
the leading international forest-certification organization. Our books carrying the FSC
label are printed on FSC®-certified paper. FSC is the only forest-certification scheme
endorsed by the leading environmental organizations, including Greenpeace. Our
paper-procurement policy can be found at www.randomhouse.co.uk/environment.

Typeset in Weiss and Mrs Eaves by Falcon Oast Graphic Art Ltd.
Printed and bound in Great Britain by
Clays Limited, Bungay, Suffolk

2 4 6 8 10 9 7 5 3 1

To the Best Beloved, for his helpful marginalia

CONTENTS

CONTENTS

ACKNOWLEDGEMENTS

Thank you to Susanna Wadeson for her enthusiastic help and support, without which I would have gone under!

Thank you to Brenda Updegraff for her very necessary, eagle-eyed editing. Thank you to Andrew Davidson for the cover illustration and to Patrick Mulrey for the illustrations inside.

Thank you to Tom Poland and to Philip Lord for the design.

And thank you to my family for their patience over the long months.

PREFACE

GROWING VEGETABLES can be puzzling for the beginner: it's often difficult to know when to plant or what to plant. This handbook is a practical, topical diary that makes it quite clear when and how to plant each crop. With up to six tasks for each month, it offers solutions to common problems and up-to-date information on varieties – plus some fascinating facts. I hope it will be equally useful to beginners and experienced vegetable-growers. Whenever there's a spare 10 minutes, use them. Some tasks inevitably take longer but much can be achieved in short bursts of activity on a regular basis.

The book is written for the gardener of today and recommends modern varieties at the forefront of plant breeding, as well as those tried and tested favourites that remain first class. All the techniques described are completely organic, because that is the way I garden. In the modern age, with fewer chemicals on offer, gardeners have to be greener. In any case, when growing food a no-chemical approach seems more sensible – after all, we are feeding ourselves, our families and our friends.

Organic gardening is nothing new. Our grandparents and ancestors were skilled in the art of vegetable-growing and they relied on good husbandry rather than a quick chemical fix. I have been growing vegetables, flowers and fruit organically for over 40 years, so I write from first-hand experience. I have made many mistakes over the years, but I'd like to think that the advice I can now pass on is highly practical.

I hope you will find this book helpful and will gain as much pleasure from gardening as I do. The joy of harvesting your own vegetables is hard to describe, but it is best shared!

Happy gardening.

Val Bourne

WINTER TASKS

To Do

Check stored vegetables
Cut pea sticks – hazel is best
Harvest winter vegetables
Complete winter digging
Spread compost
Double dig some areas
Chit early and second early
    potatoes
Force chicory
Clean pots and seed trays
Buy canes, string, labels, etc.
Check on your seeds
Force rhubarb
Cloche an area where the earliest
    sowings are to be made
Track down hibernating snails

Sow Outdoors

'Aquadulce Claudia' broad beans
'Feltham First' peas

Sow under Glass

Less hardy, taller varieties of
    broad beans
Lettuce

Plant

Shallot sets
Onion sets
Some garlic varieties

JANUARY

*T*he gardening year starts here and I'm a little like Janus, the Roman god of gateways, because I look backwards and forwards at this time of year. I gloat about last year's successes, that's for sure, but I try to analyse the failures too. Was it the weather? Or did I choose the wrong variety? Or was it me? Every year is a learning curve and even experienced gardeners learn something new. Yet I always look forward to the new gardening year.

At the start of the year, the best piece of advice for the vegetable-grower is to bide your time because impatience and doing things too soon is a recipe for disaster. Timing is everything when it comes to vegetables. So wait for the weather, and if you're a new vegetable-grower, ask someone you know who's clearly getting results. They'll happily share information.

Once the days start to lengthen, get out whenever you can. I shall be there, fork in hand, for January is a month of preparation for the busy year ahead.

1 Buy and Chit Early Potatoes

(early January)

THIS is the time to buy your seed potatoes because the really popular varieties tend to sell out. All potatoes are labelled as either first early, second early or maincrop (according to when they crop) and the tubers are guaranteed to be disease-free by the growers. The first and second early varieties should be allowed to 'chit', or produce shoots, before planting. Remove them from the packaging – taking care to wash your hands afterwards because many tubers are treated with fungicide – and lay them out on large egg trays or on clean seed trays. Look for the small eyes (the indentations with tiny buds) and angle each potato so that one eye is facing upwards. Slowly (as the light levels rise) the buds will develop into small, sprouting shoots. These race away once the tubers are planted, helping the crop to develop more quickly. It isn't necessary to chit maincrop varieties, but chitted early potatoes do produce a heavier crop.

Store the trays of potatoes somewhere cool. A garden shed is ideal. However, the tubers must be kept frost-free and out of the reach of mice and rats. So make sure that your shed is secure and well insulated.

Chitting must be done in a cool position so that the sprouting growth stays compact. Too much warmth produces long, etiolated shoots that snap off as you plant. Plant them outside from mid-April onwards.

Did you know? The potato is high in vitamin C and it was a principal source during two world wars, so much so that when the crop failed in 1916 scurvy broke out among the army. A medium helping of new potatoes will give you half your daily vitamin C allowance.

Organic Tip ✔

Do grow your own. Commercial crops of potatoes are frequently sprayed against blight. The 'Sarpo' varieties (bred from wild solanum species originally collected by the Russian geneticist Nikolai Vavilov around 1925) are selected for total blight resistance.

SECRETS OF SUCCESS

- Gamble and plant four or five tubers now, protecting them with plastic or glass cloches. Plant a few earlies in March (see page 46), keeping the rest of your chitted tubers until mid–late April.
- Potatoes are very susceptible to frost damage. Earth your early potatoes up (i.e., mound soil over most of the emerging growth), covering the new foliage, to protect the vulnerable shoots. If a cold night is forecast, fleece your crop.

FIRST EARLY VARIETIES

'Foremost' AGM
White, firm, oval tubers.

'Red Duke of York' AGM
A red-skinned, floury, yellow-fleshed
potato. Best steamed.

'Accent' AGM
Yellow, round potatoes. Excellent eaten
cold.

SECOND EARLY VARIETIES

'Lady Cristl'
Bulks up very well. Always early. Oval,
creamy tubers with a firm texture. Eel-
worm resistant.

'Nadine'
A handsome, waxy, cream potato. Good to
eat and exhibit.

'Charlotte'
Yellow-skinned, waxy tubers. First-rate
flavour.

'Belle de Fontenay'
Also sown as maincrop. A heritage
French creamy potato producing dogleg-
shaped tubers. Bakes brilliantly, but
susceptible to blight.

For further varieties, see August, page
118 and September, page 143.

2 Double Digging
(early January)

CROPS DO best on well-fed garden soil. The compost from your
heap is airy and fertile, and this is the time to dig it out. However,
most heaps never get hot enough to kill off all the seeds that
inevitably congregate. When the compost is spread over the soil
surface, seeds germinate and, sadly, they are normally weeds. So
the best way to incorporate well-rotted compost and avoid the
problem of weeds appearing is to bury it a spit (or a spade's depth)
below the soil surface. This is called 'double digging' and the words

do sound ominous. However, you will only need to double dig each area once every three to four years, and in any case by January most gardeners are normally straining at the leash to get outside and take some exercise.

You will need a sharp spade, a fork, a wheelbarrow, a line and a groundsheet. A stout plank to stand on, so that you don't compress the soil, is also an essential.

Section off a 2.4m by 1.2m (8ft by 4ft) area of garden. Lay the sheet down on the left-hand side if you're right-handed. With your spade, remove a spit of soil from the entire area and heap it up tidily on the sheet. You will end up with a neat, flat-bottomed trough in the ground and a pile of soil by the side. Take your fork and break up the ground at the base of the trench, then incorporate your garden compost, well-rotted manure or a mixture of both into the ground. Then replace all the soil to form a flat-topped mound. The decomposition process carries on, warming the soil and helping your crops to grow. The '8 by 4' bed is small enough to make double digging, and planting, quick and easy.

Did you know? For centuries horse dung was always considered to be the finest animal manure. Arab gardeners, who first used hotbeds over 1,000 years ago, fed their best horses with a special diet of barley, beans and alfalfa to produce superior, nitrogen-rich manure.

EQUIPMENT

A stainless-steel spade, a strong fork and a line for measuring.

A decent, light wheelbarrow.

A waterproof groundsheet and wellingtons.

Regular cups of tea or coffee, hopefully provided by someone who will admire your work.

SECRETS OF SUCCESS

- You can double dig only in good weather when the ground is on the dry side. Then every spade of soil is lighter.
- A good compost heap with a lift-off front is essential so that you can remove a wheelbarrow of compost easily. Don't overfill the barrow.
- Pace yourself – there is no rush – and think of the increase in yield that your double digging will bring about.

3 Winter Care of Brassicas
(mid-January)

BRASSICAS are the gardener's standby in winter. They provide months of food, but they do need the cold weather to develop their distinctive sweet flavour. You can emulate the cold process by picking Brussels sprouts (or any other brassica) and storing them in the fridge for 10 days.

The hardiest of all are probably the kales, which will survive even in savage winters. The green curly kale can be picked from October through to spring and there is also a red version, 'Redbor'. The slender-leaved Tuscan varieties, like 'Cavolo de Nero', are just as hardy as the others. Red cabbage will also shrug off the weather well. These toughies should always be grown.

Brussels sprouts and purple sprouting broccoli can succumb in hard winters, so tidy up all fallen leaves now because they can harbour disease and shelter slugs. Remove any cabbage stumps, or any Brussels plants that have finished cropping. If you haven't netted against pigeons, do so now. They will be at their most voracious in March, just when the purple sprouting broccoli is budding up. You may have to knock snow off the net.

All brassicas require a great deal of nitrogen. It's traditional to plant them in a plot that was occupied by legumes the year before, because the nodules on the roots of peas and beans fix nitrogen into the soil naturally. Onions and shallots usually follow brassicas and these shallow-rooted, bulbous vegetables are also quite greedy feeders, so dose the soil with blood, fish and bone (a slow-release fertilizer; see page 158) as you remove old brassica plants.

Did you know? The Brussels sprout was first recorded in Brussels in 1750 and is thought to have been a natural hybrid related to wild kale. Sprouts became popular in Britain about 100 years later, but the tall varieties bred in the late nineteenth century have been superseded by shorter modern FI hybrids that button up all along the stem.

SECRETS OF SUCCESS

• See page 55.

Organic Tip ✔

Perhaps the most widespread predator of the Cabbage White caterpillar is a tiny wasp called Cotesia glomerata. *It lays eggs into the caterpillars as they emerge from the egg cases. The wasp larvae develop inside the growing caterpillars and eventually burst out of their bodies and almost immediately form sulphur-yellow cocoons. These resemble yellow rock wool and this can be seen in nooks and crannies — often in the greenhouse. Should you spot any, leave the cocoons to develop.*

VARIETIES

Kale 'Dwarf Green Curled'
Very crinkled leaves on compact plants (up to 40cm/16in). A superfood, although once despised as a poor man's crop. October–April.

Red Cabbage 'Red Jewel' F1 AGM
Large, tightly packed hearts of crisp, ruby-red leaves. Stands and stores well. Cut after Christmas.

Kale 'Cavolo de Nero'
Slender, dark-green leaves that can be harvested from late autumn right through the year. Handsome on the plot.

Brussels Sprout 'Bosworth' AGM
Mid-season sprout with firm, smooth, dark-green buttons well spaced on the stem. Stands well in winter.

---

4 Prepare for Seed-Sowing
(mid-January)

WASHING pots and seed trays could never be described as exciting. It's definitely a job for a bright day and the radio does help. But hygiene is important in seed-sowing and this is one of few times of year when you can tackle it.

Brush the debris off trays and pots. Wipe them over with a damp cloth and immerse them in a bowl of hot water, then take up the scourer. Allow yourself a dab of washing-up liquid. Lay the trays outside on a bright day, rinse them with a hose and let them drain and dry before stacking them.

If investing in some new pots or trays, choose smooth-sided and -bottomed ones with no indentations. Make sure there is no lip on the edges. Trays like this provide little or no opportunity for slugs to sleep under or near your seedlings.

Once you start sowing, always water seedlings with mains water using a can with a fine rose. Use at least two cans if possible and when you empty one, fill it up and allow it to stand for several hours. This will warm up the water and allow chlorine to escape. The rose should be facing upwards to allow the water to fall as a fine rain. Try to water before midday, ventilate the greenhouse or shed, then fill both cans and shut them inside.

Did you know? 'Watering pots', usually with handles on the top, were used by gardeners for centuries. The earliest known appearance of the term 'watering can' was in the 1692 diary of the keen Cornish gardener Lord Timothy George. In 1886 the Haws company patented a new design with a single round handle at the rear. This soon became the established shape for all watering cans and has remained so, with little variation, ever since.

KNOW YOUR COMPOSTS

John Innes is a loamy recipe not a brand.

Nos 1, 2 and 3 contain the same ingredients, but the amount of food differs.

No. 1 is for pricking out seedlings.

No. 2 is for potting on seedlings.

No. 3 is for mature plants and for gross feeders like tomatoes.

Most composts contain only enough food to last for up to 6 weeks; after that the food runs out.

Use seed-sowing compost for seed.

Organic Tip ✔

Resist the urge to use Jeyes Fluid, bleach or any other chemical cleaner. These are damaging to the environment and will harm many of your overwintering friendly predators.

SECRETS OF SUCCESS

- Water is the undoing of most gardeners when it comes to seed-sowing. Don't over-water seedlings – put your index finger in the compost and sense how damp it is.
- Use the correct compost for seed-sowing. Mixtures are usually fluffy and light, but sifting the compost through your fingers adds more air.
- Water the compost before you sow.
- Always use mains water; water-butt water is less hygienic.

---

5 Sow Broad Beans under Glass

(late January)

RAISE YOUR broad bean plants under glass (in a cool greenhouse or cold frame) ready for planting out in March or early April. The cooler temperatures at this time of year encourage good root systems. You can sow two types – the taller, long-podded varieties and the shorter, hardier 'Aquadulce Claudia'.

Use modules (sectioned-off seed trays) that fit inside large seed trays: the 24 size (6 × 4) is ideal. Place the module into the seed tray and fill it with seed-sowing compost. Press one seed into each module and water the whole tray well. Cover with wire if you have a mouse problem – these large seeds are a lure!

Once the young beans reach 5cm (2in) in height, plant them out as soon as possible before the long radical root gets tangled up in the hole at the bottom of the module. Space them out, one plant every 22cm (9in) with 30cm (12in) between a double row. Put a series of canes round them and add some supporting string to prevent them flopping over other crops. Always top your canes with a cap or a small flowerpot to protect your eyes from damage when you pick. Decorative cane tops – mine are harvest mice on ears of wheat – are fun.

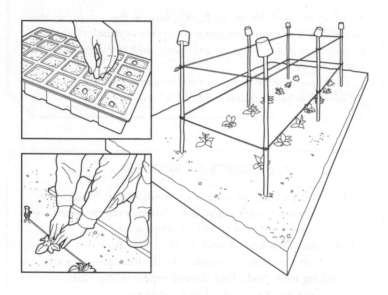

In March it's possible to sow the seeds straight into the ground. Use two seeds per hole to a depth of almost 5cm (2in). Plant a dozen extra seeds at each end of the rows for gapping up (i.e. filling any gaps in the rows). Cover with chicken wire if mice are a problem and then add canes.

Did you know? Broad beans originated in the region south of the Caspian Sea, but are now extinct in the wild. They were taken to America by the early Spanish settlers and became known as 'fava beans' from their Latin name. They didn't catch on in North America for a long time and were subsequently grown more in South America. Today Brazil is a leading exporter, but China is the world's biggest producer.

Organic Tip ✔

Broad beans inevitably attract blackfly because they emerge as these insects leave their winter host plants (Euonymus or spindle tree) to look for leafy bean plants. Pinch out and destroy any tips that get blackfly as soon as you see them.

Don't spray, even with organic mustard, garlic or soap sprays, as you will also kill helpful ladybirds and parasitic wasps.

SECRETS OF SUCCESS

- Mice and rats can devastate a row within an hour, even burrowing under snow. Keep them away by covering the seeds and plants with chicken wire.
- Once the pods are set well up the stem, pick out the tips so that the plants concentrate all their energies on filling each pod. You should expect 900g (2lb) of beans per 30cm (12in) of double row.
- Broad beans are self-fertile, but the yield is much higher when bumble bees cross-pollinate them. Wet or inclement weather can make a crop suffer because bees tend not to visit.
- Pick them regularly so that they keep producing flowers.
- Pick carefully, as broad-bean stems tend to be brittle. Use small scissors to snip off the pods if needed.

6 Make a Runner Bean Trench
(late January)

IF DOUBLE digging seems a little onerous, it is well worth restricting your efforts to making a runner bean trench in readiness for May sowings or plantings. Starting now will give you 3 months to complete it. You can add all your soft organic matter, such as vegetable and fruit peelings, leafy weeds, spent cabbage leaves, plain paper and tea bags or tea leaves, etc. – all the things that would normally go on the compost heap. You can add comfrey leaves as well as pet bedding from rabbits and guinea pigs, but not cat or dog faeces as these are acidic.

Leave the trench open. The heap inside will begin to decompose a little, but once it is covered with soil (in March) the decomposition process will speed up as warmth is generated and moisture trapped below the soil's surface, helping your beans to get a better start than in ordinary soil. You can also make trenches like this for hungry crops like squashes, pumpkins and courgettes.

It is a good idea to buy runner bean seeds now before the best varieties sell out. You can raise beans in two ways. Either sow under

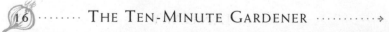

glass in April and then plant outside – no earlier than June – or plant straight into the soil from mid-May through to July (see May, page 71).

Did you know? Recently bred red-flowered runner beans ('Polestar', for instance) have greater heat tolerance than heritage red-flowered varieties like Suttons' 'Prizewinner'. This means that 'Polestar' sets more effectively even if nighttime temperatures exceed 16°C (60.8°F).

Organic Tip ✔

Slugs can nip out the growing points of runner beans and then they never recover. To lure predators away, plant young lettuces under and around your tripods or rows, then frisk them every evening at dusk when slugs are at their most active. Collect any you find and dispose of them.

SECRETS OF SUCCESS

• See page 73.

VARIETIES

For varieties, see May, page 74.

FEBRUARY

*I*t's February, the days are lengthening nicely and just occasionally there's a warm glimmer of sun that manages to penetrate your clothing. That warmth goes straight through to the heart with promises of better things to come. But there's still a long way to go when it comes to ideal planting and sowing times. Watch and wait. It's much better to catch the moment than to sow too early.

Certain crops are hardy enough to plant now, including garlic, onions and shallots, but mainly the temperatures will be too low for seeds to germinate. Our ancestors were adept at warming up the soil by covering it with glass cloches and this can work very well. So if you are prepared to gamble (and early crops are always a little risky) you could cover a small area. If you are lucky enough to have a greenhouse you can start making sowings under glass.

Soil preparation and weeding are vital so that once spring comes everything is ready. The winter frosts should have broken down any rough digging, so often all that is needed is a rake to create that elusive sowing surface — the fine tilth.

1 Sow Leeks under Cover
(early February)

LEEK SEEDS can be sown under glass now. This hardy vegetable prefers to germinate in cool conditions and once the seedlings are up you don't have to worry about cold nights. However, all members of the allium or onion family are shallow-rooted. They cannot seek out moisture from the depths, so the seedlings can dry out easily. If young leeks become water-stressed they tend to bolt (run to seed), so it's vital to keep your seedlings damp. For this reason I always try to keep them out of direct sunlight in the greenhouse. Leeks can be sown outside straight into the ground if you wish, but not until mid-March at the earliest.

The easiest way to raise leeks of the right size under glass is to use 6 × 4 modules. Place two seeds in each one, then weed out the weaker seedling if necessary, leaving the other to fill the space. Once the young plants are pencil-thick (after 10 weeks or so) they are ready to go outside. Make deep holes with a dibber, drop one leek plant in each and then fill the holes with water. The tops and roots do not need trimming. Each hole needs to be 15cm (6in) deep with 22–30cm (9–12in) between each. Rows should be between 30–38cm (12–15in) apart. Wider spacings aid air flow, helping to prevent diseases like rust.

Transplanting usually takes place in the second half of May, although leeks can be planted out up until mid-July. Most of the growing takes place in autumn and leeks are invaluable – they almost always come through the hardest winters unscathed.

Did you know? The Ancient Egyptians grew leeks in the time of the pharaohs. The Greeks and Romans also loved them. Nero was said to eat them with olive oil to preserve his voice. The leek has a powerful reputation as a medicinal plant and it was also thought to have magical properties. If you wore a leek it would protect you from battle wounds, stop you from being struck by lightning and keep away evil spirits.

Organic Tip ✔

Leeks do not do well on compacted soil, so adding some well-rotted organic matter really helps this crop dramatically. Keep the weeds down – but remember those shallow roots.

SECRETS OF SUCCESS

- Fork over the soil a day or two before planting; this makes it easier to get the dibber in.
- Choose a good F1 variety for early sowing – the seeds germinate better.
- Once the seedlings have been 'dibbed in', water the whole plot well and keep it damp. Don't dribble on water; use a sprinkler if possible and give the whole area a thorough soaking for at least 2 hours in the latter half of the day.
- Continue to water in this way whenever dry weather occurs in the first month after planting. Once they look established, leave them to their own devices.
- Lift leeks as you need them, using a fork, as they are best eaten very fresh. They will not store for long: they become tough.
- If a leek bolts, snap off the flowering stem.
- You can earth leeks up to blanch more stem.

'Oarsman' AGM
A smooth-skinned, maincrop F1 hybrid leek that is much kinder on the stomach than the thickly textured, cellulose-packed 'Musselburgh'. Long, sleek shanks that cook sweetly.

'Carlton' AGM
An earlier F1 variety producing mid- to dark-green flags, but this variety bolts more easily than some so is not for dry gardens.

'King Richard' AGM
An early, pale-green variety that resists bolting well.

'Apollo' AGM
Vigorous plants with attractive dark-green leaves that fan out from a thick white shank. Ready from mid–late winter and resistant to rust.

2 Plant Garlic
(early February)

GARLIC IS another shallow-rooted member of the allium family that needs lots of water to crop well. In the wild this plant from the high mountains is woken up by melting snow and warmer temperatures. Hot, dry weather triggers dormancy and, as a gardener, you should be harvesting once the leaves begin to wither and yellow.

There are two types of garlic – softneck and hardneck. The softnecks produce plump, white bulbs and, if planted now, they can be harvested from mid-July and will keep until April. Softnecks tend to bulb up as the days shorten after the summer solstice. Hardneck cultivars produce an edible flowering stalk (or rocambole) and this must be snapped off as soon as it emerges to encourage the bulb to swell. Their flavour is stronger and the bulbs are usually more colourful. Hardnecks are planted in September and October and harvested in June. They generally keep until January.

The planting technique is the same for both. Break the bulb into cloves just before planting and place the individual cloves

2.5–5cm (1–2in) below the soil surface, roughly 15cm (6in) apart. Lift and harvest as soon as the leaves begin to yellow.

Did you know? Egyptian slaves were given a daily ration of garlic to ward off illness and increase strength and endurance. During the reign of Tutankhamen 7kg (15lb) of garlic would buy a healthy slave.

SECRETS OF SUCCESS

- A sunny site is vital for garlic.
- Don't try to grow supermarket garlic: invest in proper varieties.
- Snap off any flowering stalks if they appear on hardneck varieties: this will fatten the bulbs.
- Water is vital for large, plump bulbs.
- Dry the bulbs thoroughly before storing or plaiting.

SOFTNECK VARIETIES

'Venetian Wight' (from the Po Valley in Italy)
Small, hard, white garlic that will keep until spring. Intense flavour and quite hot.

'Provence Wight' (from the Drôme Valley in Provence)
Grows well in Britain and the fat, juicy cloves are perfect for adding some Mediterranean flavour to vegetable and fish dishes. Can also be planted in autumn.

'Solent Wight' (from the Auvergne in France)
The most robust garlic in overall terms of eating and keeping. Large, dense white bulbs with a good flavour. The easiest garlic to plait.

'Tuscany Wight' (from Italy)
Large, fat cloves all the way round the bulb. Classic Italian flavour, good with chicken and lentils.

For more garlic varieties, see August, page 116.

Organic Tip ✔

Always lift garlic as soon as you spot the leaves fading or yellowing, otherwise the bulbs will sprout again and will be no good for storing.

3 Cloche Areas Ready for Sowing

(mid-February)

OUR ANCESTORS were far more inventive than we are when it came to growing vegetable and fruit crops, and they used protective glass in a variety of ways to produce precocious crops. We, however, have a whole range of products that weren't available to them. They include child-friendly plastic, horticultural fleece, Ecomesh and all sorts of netting.

Now that the February sun is beginning to gain some warmth, it's possible to cloche some areas where early crops will be sown. These might include carrots, parsnips, beetroot and spinach. Lightweight polythene cloches are not suitable for windy gardens – they do a disappearing act. Even those with holes that allow the wind to pass through tend to end up decorating the local hedgerows.

However, the heavier plastic cloches are useful for covering areas of ground will can be used for sowing. Prepare the ground well so that the soil is fine, then water it well if it is dry. Cover with your cloche, making sure the ends are blocked off. Many a cat has adopted the warm ground underneath. Open the ends regularly to allow the air to circulate. After 2 weeks sow the seeds, water again if necessary, and cover once again with the cloche. If cold weather is forecast, fleece over the plastic with a double layer.

Did you know? The giant glass belljar was introduced into Britain in the early seventeenth century and was immediately known by its French name of *cloche*. The 'big glass hats', as they were called, were covering the melon beds of England by 1629. By 1677 English-made square glazed less-breakable covers with lead frames and lids had taken over.

Organic Tip ✔

When you plant out your first courgette, squash, cucumber and pumpkin plants at the beginning of June, cloching them at night (with a sturdy plastic bell cloche or similar) produces plants double the size of the uncloched ones.

SECRETS OF SUCCESS

- Invest in sturdy materials that will last for a few seasons. Light polythene and wafer-thin plastic are not rugged enough.
- Ventilation is the key to success when covering plants, because still, damp air encourages fungal diseases like damping off and botrytis. Make time to uncover your seedlings or young plants every day, exposing them to fresh air.
- Water regularly, because rain cannot penetrate most barriers and this includes Enviromesh and horticultural fleece.
- Use wire or wood supports to keep any coverings away from the foliage. Canes can be used.
- Early strawberries can be protected with a makeshift tent covered with thick polythene.

4 Force and Divide Rhubarb

(mid-February)

OVER THE years mature rhubarb clumps can become very large and this is the best time of year to divide them, just as the large, dome-like buds are breaking dormancy. Lift the whole crown and, using a spade, split it into chunks containing four or five buds. Replant in enriched soil containing garden compost, making sure that the top of the clump is just above the ground. Do not pick any stems in the first year or two and always remove any flowering spikes.

You can force established rhubarb crowns growing in the ground by covering them with purpose-made terracotta forcers or upturned dustbins full of straw. The dark, warm conditions inside force the stems into premature growth, producing soft, pale-pink stems that have a champagne flavour when cooked.

However, once you have forced one crown it must be rested for 2–3 years and allowed to grow naturally. Some gardeners just discard the crowns they have forced. The best technique is to plant three crowns so that one is recovering from being forced the year before, one is cropping naturally and one is being forced. Then you will be able to have a supply of forced stems every year. However, the yield from forced rhubarb is roughly half that of a plant grown naturally. Expect 2.6–3.6kg (6–8lb) from forcing a decent crown.

Did you know? *Rha* was the name the Greeks gave to the River Volga and to the edible plant that grew on its banks. Later, the plant became known in Latin as *rha barbum* ('barbarian' or 'foreign') and from this the name 'rhubarb' is derived. The first forced rhubarb was an accident. Workmen at the Chelsea Physic Garden in 1815 covered the rhubarb patch with builders' rubble. When it was cleared, long, pale stems were uncovered. Commercial forcing in Yorkshire's 'Rhubarb Triangle' began in the 1880s and many of the rhubarb varieties we grow today date from this golden era. The Triangle once covered a 30-square-mile area between Leeds, Wakefield and Bradford, but now it is reduced to a 9-square-mile area between Wakefield, Morley and Rothwell.

SECRETS OF SUCCESS

- Choose an open, sunny site and prepare the soil by working in plenty of farmyard manure or compost before planting.
- Plant in spring where possible, placing new crowns 1m (3ft) apart with the buds just above the surface. Don't pull any stems until the second year of growth.
- Never cut rhubarb. The technique is to pull and then twist very gently from the lower stem.
- Stop harvesting at the end of May to allow your plants to recover.
- If a stressed plant should run to seed, remove the flowering spike straight away. Water, feed and mulch lightly.
- Tidy rhubarb in autumn so that slugs do not have anywhere to hide.

VARIETIES

'Timperley Early' AGM (early)
So early it's probably better not to force it. The slender, long, pink-red stems have a tart flavour that makes this an excellent crumble filler. Not a prolific cropper – but a must for all rhubarb lovers.

'Hawke's Champagne' AGM (early–mid season)
Delicately thin, long scarlet stems with a sweet flavour from early spring. An old variety, but easy to grow and ideal for forcing. Attractive appearance.

'Queen Victoria' (mid–late season)
Colourful, strong red stems, easy and prolific. This heritage variety still holds its own today. Vigorous, making huge clumps, so perhaps not for smaller gardens.

'Raspberry Red' (mid–late season)
An old Dutch variety, recently reintroduced, with sweeter red stems. Given a sunny, open position it is a heavy cropper.

5 Plant Shallots
(late February)

TRADITIONAL garden wisdom decrees that shallots should be planted on the shortest day and harvested on the longest because they take 24–26 weeks to mature. However, we suffer from wetter, warmer winters than we used to have and I've found that the results are much better from late-February plantings. Plant now and you can harvest in August when the weather is at its warmest.

The flavour of shallots is subtler and more aromatic than that of onions, so they are well worth growing, especially for the keen cook. However, despite being smaller in size, they actually take up more space in the garden than onions. The foliage splays outwards as the cluster of shallots forms and you should get between seven and nine babies per set. Choose a sunny position and plant them 22cm (9in) apart in rows 22cm (9in) apart. Leave the upper third of the bulb showing because shallots are prone to rotting in damp soil.

Shallots grow better and ripen better in sunnier summers and, although they are not quite as hardy as onions, they often store for longer. There are red and yellow varieties, but the yellow ones are the easiest to grow and they also store for longer. The key to good shallots is watering in the early stages and also putting them on fertile ground. Ideally, the onion plot should have been manured or enriched in the months leading up to planting.

Did you know? The botanical name for the shallot, *Allium ascalonicum*, is derived from Ascalon, a place in Palestine where shallots are thought to have originated. The Crusaders possibly brought them to England in the twelfth century, but the Greek writer Theophrastus (371–287 BC) referred to them in his writings, as did Pliny the Elder in the first century AD.

VARIETIES

'Golden Gourmet' AGM
The heaviest-cropping, golden, ball-shaped shallot, producing substantial bulbs.

'Longor' AGM
A long, slender 'Jersey long' shallot with golden skin, almost pear-shaped, with a strong flavour.

'Pikant' AGM
A Dutch variety. The best red, with lots of layers of brown-red skin and a very rounded shape. Good flavour.

'Jermor' AGM
A copper-coloured, long shallot, widely grown commercially in Brittany. Pink-tinted flesh and a good flavour.

SECRETS OF SUCCESS

- Find a garden hotspot where the sun shines and be prepared to water them well in warm, dry weather.
- Source good-quality, plump sets that feel firm to the touch and that have no mould.
- Avoid planting on newly manured ground — it scorches the roots.
- If you find shallots difficult to grow, opt for globular, golden varieties — they are the easiest to grow and they store for longer.
- The banana-shaped shallots and the red shallots do not store for as long as the yellow. If you grow them, use them up before the end of December.
- Lift the shallots away from the ground with a fork in August to help the drying-out process, gently teasing the clusters of bulbs apart.

6 Plant Onion Sets
(late February)

IT'S ALSO time to plant onion sets, and the first job is to trim off the little wispy tops with a small pair of scissors; otherwise the birds will tug them out. They should take 20 weeks to reach maturity. Later in the year (usually by mid-March), there are more-expensive, heat-treated sets for sale. These are planted in March and April and their biggest advantage is that they rarely (if ever) bolt.

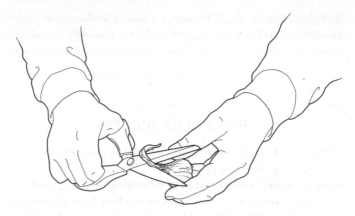

Bolting is more of a problem in areas that get dry springs and searing winds. If that describes your conditions and you've experienced lots of bolting onions, use the heat-treated sets. If bolting does occur, remove the flower bud and stem immediately.

Space your sets 15cm (6in) in rows 22cm (9in) apart. Push each set into the ground so that the tip is at ground level and use lines to keep the rows straight. It's essential to keep down the weeds with a small onion hoe, because, like shallots, onions are shallow-rooted and can't cope with competition. Having neatly aligned rows is a huge help when hoeing.

> **Did you know?** There is no wild equivalent of the onion, so it must have been domesticated for thousands of years. Carvings appear on Egyptian tombs that are 5,000 years old. When King Rameses IV died, onions were placed in the eye sockets of his mummified body as a symbol of eternal life. The Romans are credited with bringing the onion to Britain.

SECRETS OF SUCCESS

- Water well in the early stages whenever the soil is dry to develop the root system.
- Keep onion beds well weeded by hoeing them regularly with a small hoe. This will create a fine layer on the top which mulches the soil beneath and keeps moisture in.
- Plant onions in a bright position.
- Do not bend the necks artificially.
- In August you should be able to lift the bulbs away from the soil with a fork. A couple of weeks afterwards it's possible to lay the onions on their sides.
- Laying onion bulbs on a simple framework will dry them for storage.

VARIETIES

'Sturon' AGM
A globe-shaped, yellow-brown onion with juicy flesh. Produces rounded, medium-sized bulbs quickly and rarely bolts.

'Red Baron' AGM
A dark, glossy, red-skinned onion with sweet flesh and a good flavour. Still the best red variety.

'Centurion' AGM
A golden onion with a flattened shape and a distinctive pale skin the colour of straw. A heavy yielder with a crisp flavour.

'Santero'
A new, downy, mildew-resistant F1 onion with coppery-brown skin. Good in the drier parts of the country where mildew is prevalent.

SPRING TASKS

To Do

Prepare soil for planting

Fertilize with blood, fish and bone (see page 158) or powdered or pelleted chicken manure

Keep weeding

Water on slug nematodes in key areas

Put up bean canes

Protect early sowings of potatoes by earthing them up (i.e. mounding soil up around plants, leaving just the tops showing) or covering them with fleece

Harden off tender plants before planting

Fleece vulnerable plants on cold nights

Remove and clear all winter vegetables

Uncover rhubarb crowns that have been forced

●●●●●●●●●●●●●●●●●●●●●●●●●●●●●●●●

Sow Outdoors

Beetroot

Carrot

Spinach

Broad beans

Peas

Parsnips

Turnips

Swede

Sow under Glass

Leeks
Sweet and chilli peppers
Tomatoes
Aubergines
Cucurbits – cucumber, squash,
    pumpkin, courgette, etc.
Lettuce
Brussels sprouts, purple
    sprouting broccoli, kale,
    cabbages
Runner and French beans
Sweetcorn
Celery
Chicory and endive
Herbs
Globe artichokes

Plant

Asparagus crowns
Potatoes
Rhubarb
Broad beans grown in modules

•••••••••••••••••••••••••••••••

MARCH

In theory, March is the month when spring arrives, but the weather is never predictable and, as timing is everything when it comes to gardening, this should be the month for watching and waiting for the right growing conditions. Sow too early, when the soil is still cold and wet, and your crops will sit there and fail. Bide your time and go with the weather, not the calendar. This may be frustrating, but years of experience have taught me the wisdom behind the proverb 'Patience is a virtue' when it comes to growing vegetables.

March days can be warm, but nighttime temperatures usually plummet and there are still several weeks when frost may strike, so the crops that are planted during March have to be totally hardy. Tender crops (including tomatoes, peppers, cucurbits and aubergines) are best left until later in the season. Even a slight frost will kill them. Also, their growth can be permanently checked by cool nights and checked plants do not generally recover. You can start seeds and young plants off in a warm greenhouse in March, but don't venture outside with tender crops until mid-May.

1 Sow Early Peas
(early March)

ALWAYS assess the condition of your soil before sowing early crops. If the soil sticks to your boots it is too wet to plant or sow, so turn your attention to verges and edges. Using a moon-shaped cutter, angle the tool slightly outwards rather than straight down. This exaggerates the edge and makes it look deeper. It also improves drainage and helps to prevent weed seeds congregating in the groove at the bottom. Neatening the edges and weeding all furrows will improve the appearance of your plot greatly and prevent the weeds from self-seeding.

When sowing your peas take heed of the old adage 'One for the mouse, one for the crow, one to rot and one to grow' and use lots of seeds. Make a 22cm (9in) wide shallow trench and zigzag the seeds across it from side to side. Cover the seeds with 2.5cm (1in) of soil and then cover the soil with wire netting to keep birds and mice away. Add twiggy supports straight after sowing – hazel is best – setting them along each side of the trench, about 20cm (8in) apart and at an angle, so that their tops meet over the trench and the pea shoots will weave through them.

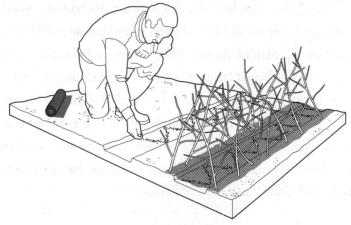

'Feltham First' is the best early pea variety and will reach only 40cm (16in). Mangetout varieties can also be sown now. Maincrops can be sown by mid-April. On average, peas take 100 days to mature and regular fortnightly sowings of taller, maincrop varieties can be made right up until late July.

EARLY VARIETIES

Paler, round peas with a floury flavour and grainy texture.

'Misty' AGM
A good cropper with blunt-ended, smaller pods each containing six peas.

'Early Onward' AGM
A heavy early cropper with pairs of pods.

'Feltham First'
For autumn or spring sowing, this round-seeded variety produces a substantial crop.

MANGETOUT VARIETIES

The pods are picked and eaten young – before the peas develop.

'Oregon Sugar Pod' AGM
Matures first and produces sweet, juicy pods for lightly steaming or stir-frying.

'Delikata' AGM
Taller and heavier-cropping than 'Oregon Sugar Pod', but gets stringy quickly.

MAINCROP VARIETIES

Sweetly succulent, bright-green peas that melt in the mouth.

'Jaguar' AGM
Ready after 100 days with short pods containing seven peas.

'Cavalier' AGM
British-bred, with pairs of long, straight pods containing nine peas. Good flavour.

'Hurst Green Shaft' AGM
Tried and tested heavy-cropper that produces long, easily picked pods. Rarely fails.

Organic Tip ✔

Peas (like all legumes) should never be given a nitrogen-rich feed. They fix their own nitrogen by forming an association with certain bacteria.

SECRETS OF SUCCESS

- Peas like cool, moist conditions and often do best in cooler summers.
- They should be watered well at least once a week in dry weather as soon as they come into flower.
- Pick regularly to encourage more pods.
- Always sow a late crop in late July — they often do very well.

2 Sow Globe Artichokes
(early March)

THESE HIGHLY ornamental Mediterranean sun-lovers produce edible flower buds which can be harvested in early summer when little else is available to the vegetable gardener. Pick before the blue petals start to show, then simmer in water and douse them in butter for a quick and appetizing 'plot-to-plate' lunch. Alternatively, leave them alone so that they develop their cobalt-blue, bee-pleasing flowers.

Globe artichokes, commonly called cardoons, often succumb in cold winters. By early March you will be able to tell which of last year's crop have survived and which have died. Dig up any dead plants, clean away the debris and fill the gaps with offsets removed from your survivors. Use a sharp knife to slice the new outer shoots off below the ground. Each viable piece should have some root. Pot them up and give them 6 weeks in the warmest, lightest place you have. Bed them out once well rooted.

This is also a good time to think about sowing artichoke seeds. Sow two seeds into each small pot of compost; once germinated, select the best and bed out. If you have unheated glass you can do this in early March, or you can wait for 4 weeks and place the pots outside. Young plants can also be ordered now for May dispatch.

VARIETIES

'Concerto' F1
A new, vigorous variety with purple-washed, jade-green heads.

'Green Globe Improved'
Available as seed, this prolific variety produces less prickly heads.

'Imperial Star'
A highly selected seed strain from 'Green Globe'.

'Violetta di Chioggia'
Deep-purple-headed variety. Early, very ornamental and ready by June.

'Gros Vert de Laon'
A heritage French variety with the largest green heads and the best finely cut foliage.

SECRETS OF SUCCESS

- Globe artichokes demand a sheltered, sunny position and well-drained soil.
- These tall plants also need space to do well: thinning the stems to two or three per plant can make them easier to manage and less likely to topple over.
- Stake in windy gardens.

Did you know? The Greeks and the Romans both ate globe artichokes. The names *kardos* (Greek) and *carduus* (Latin) both translate as 'thistle'. The Romans believed this plant had aphrodisiac qualities and they imported them from Cordoba in Spain in large numbers. Henry VIII grew them at New Hall in Essex in 1530 – possibly for the same reason – but in his day women and people of low birth were not allowed to eat them. They were literally forbidden fruit.

3 Sow Three Varieties of Lettuce
(mid-March)

SELECT THREE different types of lettuce to extend the picking season. Choose a loose-leaf 'pick and come again' variety like 'Salad Bowl Mixed': this soft mixture of red and green oak leaves will be ready to pick after 8 weeks. Sow a small, hearting lettuce like 'Little Gem' or its red-leaved equivalent, 'Dazzle': these will be ready to cut 2–3 weeks later. Finally, sow a slower-maturing Cos variety like 'Lobjoits Green', which often takes 10–12 weeks to fill out.

Always use fresh packets of seeds with the correct date because lettuce has a short period of viability – 3 years at most.

Write out the labels before you start and fill the trays with compost to within 1cm (½in) of the rim. Water well with mains water before sowing. Ideally, the water should stand in a fine-rose can for at least half a day to warm up and release some of its chlorine. Using tapwater (i.e., not water from a water butt) prevents damping off – a fungal disease.

Sprinkle the pale seeds very thinly on the compost and cover lightly with a fine layer of compost. Place in a cold frame, or in an unheated greenhouse, or on a cool windowsill. Ideally, seeds will germinate within 6–14 days in reasonable temperatures.

Prick out when two proper leaves show and then plant outside once large enough. Repeat the process every 4 weeks until late July to ensure a long supply of salad leaves.

VARIETIES

'Little Gem' AGM
The best early small lettuce. It hearts up well.

'Dazzle'
Similar in shape to 'Little Gem' but with burgundy leaves.

'Salad Bowl Mixed' AGM
An early cropper, this decorative green-and-red oak-leaved lettuce is a loose-leaf variety.

'Lobjoit's Green Cos' AGM
Large, crisp, green-leaved Cos. Suitable for spring and autumn sowing.

'Nymans'
A medium-sized, shiny-leaved, red Cos lettuce. Slow to bolt (run to seed).

'Romaine'
Survives hot summers and produces crisp, dark-green, solid hearts. Traditionally used in Caesar salads.

Organic Tip ✔

Lettuces attract slugs, but if you grow African marigolds close to them or among them the marigolds act as slug magnets. Collect them at dusk and exterminate!

SECRETS OF SUCCESS

- Lettuce is a cool-season crop and most varieties struggle to germinate and grow in hot conditions.
- Sow on cooler days, or in the evenings if the weather's hot.
- Grow a selection. Lettuces mature at different rates and some (such as Cos) varieties are much less likely to bolt. Once planted out, always water in dry weather to prevent bolting.

4 Sow Tender Vegetables under Cover

(mid-March)

TENDER VEGETABLES like aubergines, chillies, peppers, squashes and tomatoes to grow outdoors can be sown under cover now. Put them in a greenhouse or on a sunny windowsill and keep the pots warm. Ideally, aubergines and peppers need temperatures above 15°C (59°F) in order to germinate within 10 days.

Large cucurbit seeds (like cucumber, courgette and squash) should be sown vertically (with the sharp end down – the root emerges from the pointy end), as they can rot easily if laid flat in the compost. These easily handled seeds can be sown straight into pots. Smaller seeds (like tomatoes and peppers) can be sown in pots or trays and then pricked out as soon as two true leaves have appeared. Use multipurpose compost or John Innes No. 2. Loosen with a small dibber and handle by the leaves, not the stem. Firm them in gently and water well. Thereafter water sparingly to encourage deep root systems. Use warm cans of tapwater (not from a water butt) to prevent fungal diseases such as damping off. Each seedling should take 5–8 weeks to develop into a proper plant.

Keep seed trays under cover (or somewhere very sheltered) until early June, and cover with thick horticultural fleece if a cool night is forecast. Remove it during the day.

As soon as plants come into flower, start to water on a high-potash tomato feed every 2 weeks to encourage flowers and fruit. Keep feeding your plants until the beginning of September to keep them productive.

SECRETS OF SUCCESS

- Frost-tender plants need raising in the greenhouse, or buy them from garden centres. Harden them off carefully before putting outside.
- Plant outside once the fear of frost has passed. June is always better than May because the slightest frost can blacken and kill young courgettes, cucumbers and squashes. Cold nights will also check the growth of tomatoes, peppers and aubergines.
- Water all these plants regularly in the early evening or early morning.
- Feed aubergines, peppers and tomatoes with a high-potash tomato feed every 2 weeks. Cucurbits do best on pelleted chicken manure.
- Squashes must be stored for 6 weeks before you eat them. This allows the starch to turn to sugar.

VARIETIES

Aubergine
'Bonica' AGM
The easiest variety, producing large, dark fruits. Needs a bumble bee for pollination.

Chilli Pepper
'Hungarian Hot Wax' AGM
Conical yellow fruits that ripen to red. Good to eat raw and also for cooking, although flavour intensifies.

Courgette
'Romanesco'
Nutty Italian courgette with ridged green fruits. 'El Greco' AGM (smooth, non-prickly, dark green), 'Soleil' AGM (slender yellow) and 'Venus' AGM (compact green) are also excellent.

Squash
'Sunshine' (All-American Winner)
A small (up to 2kg/4lb), orange, pumpkin-shaped winter squash with a chestnut flavour – similar to 'Potimarron' (up to 4kg/8lb) and 'Uchiki Kuri' (2.5kg/5lb). All three are much easier to grow than butternuts.

Sweet Pepper
'Bell Boy' AGM and 'Gourmet' AGM
Both block-ended, traditionally shaped peppers that turn from green to orange.

Tomato
'Gardener's Delight' AGM and 'Sungold' AGM
Both form large trusses holding lots of cherry tomatoes. 'Gardener's Delight' is red and 'Sungold' a sweet orange-yellow.

Tomato
'Tigerella'
Striped red-and-green tomato with a top flavour.

Tomato
'Beefsteak'
Large, fleshy tomato, good to eat raw or for cooking. Heavy yields in warm summers.

For varieties of courgettes, cucumber and squash, see page 62.

Organic Tip ✔

Water the pots of compost well before sowing these seeds and then water very sparingly, taking care not to soak the pot again, until the seeds have germinated. Once the seedlings appear, water in the morning (again sparingly) and fleece overnight to prevent nighttime chill.

5 Sow Carrots
(late March)

HOME-GROWN carrots eaten straight from the garden are sweet and nutty. They are poles apart from shop-bought ones so are worth growing yourself. Carrots germinate quickly once spring arrives and temperatures reach 12°C (54°F) and above. However, they fail if it's colder, so sow in March only if the weather is on your side. Your first crops should be harvestable from mid-June onwards, but some hardy varieties can be dug during winter. You can succession-sow every 14 days up to late August – although late sowings don't always succeed.

Cultivate the soil deeply before sowing, removing any stones with a rake. You can either sow rows or use the handle of a rake to make 15cm (6in) wide, 2.5cm (1in) deep trenches or 'drills'. Aim to sow thinly so that each carrot has its own space to develop and thinning will not be necessary. If you have to thin, do it on a damp day. Less disturbance will lead to fewer problems with carrot root fly because the aroma of exposed carrots attracts them. Harvest carefully and always cover up any exposed roots afterwards.

Varieties differ in root shape and colour. If you have stony soil, grow a stumpier carrot like 'Chantenay Red Cored' – one of the best earlier varieties. Cloching in early spring helps to warm the soil.

VARIETIES

'Early Nantes 2'
Long, tapered roots early in the season. A staple variety. 'Valor' AGM is a Nantes-type hybrid.

'Amsterdam Forcing 3' AGM
Smooth, blunt-ended carrots. Strong, with short foliage. The earliest variety of all.

'Chantenay Red Cored'
Red, coreless carrot with stumpy roots. Does well on stony soil.

'Purple Haze'
Smooth-skinned, slender, purple-skinned variety with a yellow middle. Does well in hot summers.

'Kingston' AGM
A late hybrid carrot for winter storage. Good colour and flavour.

'Eskimo' AGM
The best at overwintering due to its shallow crowns which stay under the ground.

SECRETS OF SUCCESS

- Carrots are umbellifers and this family (which includes parsley and parsnip) germinate only in warm conditions, so always wait for the weather.
- Make a drill and water it well. Sprinkle the seeds thinly and just cover lightly with soil. Protect with netting.
- Leave 30cm (12in) between each row, or make 15cm (6in) wide drills that don't need any thinning.
- Don't sow on newly manured ground – the carrots will fork.
- Rotate your crop to prevent a build-up of pests.
- Clear all carrots before the beginning of January as they can harbour slugs and other pests.

> **Did you know?** Carrots grow on poor, sandy soil in temperate zones all over Europe and Asia. Root colour varies in wild populations from white, purple and yellow through to orange. Dutch plant-breeders chose to cultivate orange carrots from the sixteenth century onwards to honour the House of Orange, and all orange varieties are high in carotene. Purple- and red-rooted carrots grow naturally in the Hindu Kush region of central Asia (possibly the home of the carrot) and they are more drought-tolerant and rich in anthocyanin.

6 Plant Early Potatoes
(late March)

PLANT SOME of your first early potatoes in the third week of March for a late June crop. Be prepared to protect them with thick horticultural fleece at night, however, as the slightest frost will kill off the foliage and ruin the crop.

Earth them up as a further protection. Plant the rest of your earlies by mid-April and by the time they pop through the ground the frosts should be over for the year.

Varieties range in flavour and texture from the floury to the waxy, and there are many to choose from. Some (like 'Rocket' and 'Swift') produce a crop in 10–12 weeks, but generally these fast-maturing varieties produce large, tasteless potatoes if left in the ground for longer. Waxy varieties boil well and have a distinctive flavour. Floury varieties can disintegrate when boiled and may be better steamed. Bear in mind that all these potatoes need eating fast. They will only store for a matter of weeks.

The big advantage of early potatoes is that they are easy to grow and full of flavour. They are also generally out of the ground before mid-August when potato blight usually strikes, egged on by humid conditions. Once the potatoes have been dug up, water the ground well and add a slow-release general fertilizer (such as blood, fish and bone), then plant another, different, crop such as leeks, cabbages or dwarf French beans.

VARIETIES

For varieties, see January, page 7, August, page 118, and September, page 143.

Did you know? Potatoes are natives of the high Andes and were found by the Conquistadors in 1537, then introduced into Europe in 1570. Consequently they weren't mentioned in the Bible and so were believed to be the devil's food. Catholic Ireland got round the problem by sprinkling them with holy water and planting them on God's Friday – the old name for Good Friday – a religious superstition that still prevails.

SECRETS OF SUCCESS

- Always buy early potatoes early enough to chit them. Lay them out on egg or seed trays in a light, frost-free shed so that they produce strong, short shoots. This chitting process speeds up the crop. Maincrops do not need chitting.
- Try to prepare the soil well and always plant the tubers in damp soil that has begun to warm up.
- Rotate potatoes on a 3- or 4-year system to prevent eel-worm.
- The first sign of blight (*Phytophthora infestans*) is flagging green foliage followed by spotting. If it strikes, cut back the foliage to minimize the spread and destroy it. Don't add it to the compost heap. Some potatoes have more blight-resistant tubers. For blight-resistant varieties, see page 118.

Organic Tip ✔

Chop off comfrey leaves (preferably 'Bocking 14') and place in the bottom of the potato trench before planting. As the leaves decompose they will boost the nitrogen in the soil and also add potash and potassium.

APRIL

April is the prime month to sow all your really hardy crops (carrots, beetroot, spinach, wrinkle-seeded peas and broad beans) outside. Although April is meant to be the first of Robert Herrick's 'four sweet months', it can be fickle. Sometimes it lives up to T. S. Eliot's description of it as the 'cruellest month' of all. Look to the weather and learn to recognize the signs that spring is really here by the flurry of birds feeding their young, or the sudden surge in growth. Once you see it, ride that wave of new life as enthusiastically as a surfer on a roaring wave.

Get the soil ready and rake it down to a fine tilth whenever the weather allows. Once the texture's fine enough, leave the soil to stand and settle for at least 2 or 3 days – particularly where finer seeds are to be sown. If April is still chilly, cloche the areas where you want to sow because warm soil is essential for fast germination. If April is warm, capitalize on every moment and sow or plant all your hardy crops in earnest.

1 Make a Hardy Herb Container

(early April)

NOW THAT temperatures are warming up, it's an excellent time to create a container dedicated to herbs. Place it close to the kitchen in a sunny position and stroke the aromatic foliage regularly – it is wonderfully sensual. Use rustic wicker or gunmetal-grey galvanized metal: both suit the fresh, spring-zing of aromatically pungent herbs like lavender, sage, chives, basil, mint and thyme. Opt for a moisture-retentive, soil-based compost that's not too rich in nutrients. John Innes No. 1 is ideal: it will not dry out too readily.

A 60cm (2ft) wide container, usually circular or square, can be packed with thirty or more herbs, or you can plant a small wicker basket instead. The trick is to mix the textures and go for lower-growing varieties. Seek out some fine-leaved thymes. Add a prostrate rosemary to flow over the edge. Then select some larger, rounder leaves, including basil and sage. Both come in a variety of colours. 'Icterine' is a variegated golden sage, 'Purpurea' is a faded-damson and 'Tricolor' is a bold combination of green, purple and cream. Thymes and mints are equally diverse and some are lemon-scented whilst others are highly pungent. Go for crinkly parsley and lots of marjoram. Unite the planting with potfuls of upright chives randomly used throughout – then your container will satisfy the palate and look stylish. Order from an organic herb specialist (like Jekka McVicar), as the range and quality will be better.

Did you know? Aromatic herbs like sage and marjoram produce flowers that are very attractive to bees. Their nectar is highly concentrated. The most concentrated of all is the nectar of marjoram, *Origanum vulgare*, which contains 76 per cent sugar. August–flying butterflies adore it too.

SECRETS OF SUCCESS

- Pack the plants in tightly – this will look better and conserve moisture. Put the lowest-growing plants (like thymes) at the front.
- Water regularly for the first month until the plants are established, then cut down on the watering.
- Take cuttings of sages, thymes and oregano.
- Snip leaves and stems with scissors when harvesting.
- Remove and either pot up or compost the plants at the end of the year and clean the container ready for next year.

VARIETIES

Narrow-leaved Sage (*Salvia lavandulifolia*)
Small, narrow leaves and a neat habit make this the ideal sage for mixed planting.

Broad-leaved Thyme (*Thymus pulegioides*)
Strongly flavoured, dark leaves and pink flowers. Less twiggy than many thymes, so easier to prepare.

Garlic Chives (*Allium tuberosum*)
A late-flowering, white-flowered chive with a gentle growth habit. Mild garlic–onion flavour.

French Tarragon (*Artemisia dracunculus*)
The best herb for chicken, with narrow, linear leaves flavoured with aniseed. Take cuttings, as it hates wet winters, but it is hardier than most books imply.

2 Sow Sweetcorn
(early April)

SWEETCORN used to be a trial to grow in years gone by and results were always poor. However, the modern F1 varieties are bred for cooler climates and will perform well if sown under cover now. Their hybrid nature makes them more vigorous and willing to crop. It also improves germination, so do opt for one of these.

Varieties are divided according to sweetness, with some listed as supersweet and some tendersweet. Each plant should produce two cobs, but once they are harvested the sugars quickly turn to starch. Make sure that your home-grown sweetcorn goes straight from plot to plate: then it will be much better than cobs bought from the supermarket. Supersweet varieties keep their sweetness for longer.

Sweetcorn has brittle roots and great care must be taken when handling plants. It's best to raise individual modules or pots to limit root disturbance. The seeds are large enough to handle individually. Almost fill the pots or modular trays with seed compost. Place one large seed in each, about 2cm (1in) deep. Water well, keep the seeds warm and they should germinate within 2 weeks. When the individual plants are 10–15cm (4–6in) high, harden them off for a week by putting your pots or trays outside. This will toughen up the foliage so that it is less attractive to slugs. Carefully plant them outside in blocks from mid-May onwards. These wind-pollinated plants need to be close together in order to produce cobs, so don't plant them in a row.

> **Did you know?** The Iroquois tribe gave the first recorded sweetcorn ('Papoon') to European settlers in 1779. They had developed a 'three sisters' system of growing squash, beans and maize together on a mound — an early example of companion planting. The beans fixed nitrogen into the soil, making it more fertile, and they used the maize for supports. The squashes covered the ground, keeping the moisture in and preventing weeds from germinating.

SECRETS OF SUCCESS

- Choose a sunny, warm position that isn't too windy.
- Plant carefully, leaving 45cm (18in) between plants, preferably on fertile ground.
- Plant outside only once the fear of frost has passed, after mid-May.
- Water thoroughly throughout the growing season to encourage large cobs.
- Tap the upper stems to spread the pollen.
- Harvest once the beard (the hairy bit at the top) is brown. If in doubt, squeeze a kernal: if a milky liquid oozes out, it's ripe.

Organic Tip ✔

Don't put your sweetcorn outside too early in the year: this is a warm-season crop that is checked by cold spring nights. Planting through black plastic helps to conserve moisture and warm the soil, leading to improved yields.

3 Sow Winter Brassicas
(mid-April)

IT'S TIME to sow brassicas for winter use and this includes purple sprouting broccoli, kale and Brussels sprouts. You can create a seed bed outside and then plant, but it's far easier to raise individual young brassica plants under glass and then harden them off and plant them out. The most efficient way is to use modular trays large enough to accommodate a 7.5cm (3in) high plant. Use just one seed per module, because brassicas are good at germinating. They appear within 2 weeks and very few seeds fail.

Grow the plants on until they are between 10cm (4in) and 12.5cm (5in) in height (this usually takes 5 weeks), then harden them off for a week by putting them outside. Protect them from pigeon attack with wire. If they get short of food and water at this stage it will hamper their development for ever. Plant them into firm, but fertile ground as soon as possible. A dusting of blood, fish and bone (see page 158) helps to supply extra nitrogen. If the weather is dry, water the plants in well.

Brussels sprouts need the most space, with 60 cm (2ft) between plants. This allows enough light for the buttons to

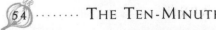

develop properly. Kale and purple sprouting broccoli can be spaced 45cm (18in) apart. Net with small-mesh butterfly netting straight after planting to prevent Small and Large Cabbage White butterflies from laying any eggs.

Organic Tip ✔

Our common wasp is the most efficient of predators. They will tackle fully grown Cabbage White caterpillars by carving them into pieces. If caterpillars do infiltrate under your netting, remove it and allow predators a couple of days to attack. Do not use wasp traps: these creatures are meat-eating bees.

SECRETS OF SUCCESS

- Sow in April in modular trays.
- Get your plants in the ground before their growth spurt stops. Don't leave them lingering in trays to get stunted and starved.
- Fertile, nitrogen-rich soil is vital for brassicas. For this reason, many gardeners grow cabbages after legumes (beans and peas) as the roots of legumes fix extra nitrogen in the soil.
- If you haven't enriched the soil, add pelleted or powdered chicken manure or blood, fish and bone at 60g (2½oz) per square metre (10–11 square feet) before planting out.
- Wild brassicas tend to grow on sandy soil near the coast, so their cultivated cousins can cope surprisingly well in warm, dry summers.
- Netting brassicas with proper butterfly netting capable of keeping out smaller butterflies is vital, as this is the only organic way to prevent caterpillars from eating the leaves.

VARIETIES

Kale
'Cavolo Nero' (Black Tuscan Kale)
This hardy kale has long, linear leaves that can be picked in autumn long before the others.

Brussels Sprout
'Bosworth' F1
A mid-season sprout that can be picked before Christmas, although it stands well into winter. Not too tall and with a good flavour.

4 Sow Beetroot, Spinach, etc.
(mid-April)

FIND SOME space to sow some edible and ornamental members of the beet family now that the soil is finally warming up. These include beetroot, spinach, Swiss chard, sea kale beet and leaf beet. All five will need to be kept well watered in their early stages to prevent bolting. Apart from this, they are all easy to grow.

Beetroot, which was grown by the Ancient Egyptians on the banks of the Nile, enjoys warm conditions and moisture. However, 'Boltardy' AGM is more tolerant of extremes of temperature, so it can be sown before any others. It produces round, smooth-skinned, dark roots. The F1 hybrid 'Alto' is also excellent and its long, cylindrical roots push above the soil surface, clearly showing the size of the root. Earth them up if slugs are a problem.

Beetroot seeds resemble small sputniks and each one produces several seedlings – so sow thinly. You can use a narrow or a wide drill and the leafy thinnings can be eaten. There are monogerm varieties that produce one plant per seed, but cropping can be poor.

Leaf beet (which comes in vivid colours) has edible stems and leaves, and the white-stemmed sea kale beet is extremely hardy. Both should overwinter if sown between April and June. Spinach can be sown in any gap up to late August to produce a quick crop. Good AGM varieties include 'Scenic' and 'Toscane' for early sowing and 'Triathlon' and 'Spokane' for late sowing.

SECRETS OF SUCCESS

- Try to emulate the conditions on the Nile (as far as possible) with warmth and moisture. Always sow in warm, moist weather. If your garden is dry, plant 'Boltardy' beetroot. This bolt-resistant variety is capable of surviving dry, cold springs.
- Choose a warm, sunny position.
- Spinach is a great gap filler and can be sown until mid-August (perhaps later) and still crop within 10 weeks.
- Repeat-sow beetroot until July, as needed.

VARIETIES

Beetroot
'Alto' F1 AGM
The sausage-shaped, tender, sweet beetroot for slicing. This longer variety pushes upwards as it develops so you can see when to harvest. Produces an early crop.

Beetroot
'Boltardy' AGM
The spherical red beetroot for succession sowing – the most popular variety of all and deservedly so.

Spinach
'Tetona' F1 AGM
A heavy-cropping spinach with smooth, green leaves. Slow to bolt, and ideal for baby leaves or for cooking. Excellent downy-mildew resistance, so good for spring and autumn sowing.

Swiss Chard
'Bright Lights'
Colourful stems in red, yellow and orange, topped by red-tinted, edible leaves make this a dual-purpose vegetable, although stems and leaves should be cooked separately.

Sow beetroot thinly and thin out if needed once the seedlings get to 7.5cm (3in). Give them space to fill out. A crowded row never works. When pulling, take beetroot from all along the row to allow those left to fatten up.

5 Apply Slug Nematodes
(late April)

TACKLE the slug and snail problem proactively now by watering on nematodes (tiny parasitic worms) in your key areas: your runner-bean patch or your hosta bed, for instance. Aim for a damp day and apply the nematodes after 4 p.m. to allow them the maximum chance of penetrating the soil effectively. One application in late April or early May (on damp soil) will solve your slug problem for 6 weeks or more – but most die underground, so the evidence will be scant. The nematodes are easy to apply: simply use a watering can with a coarse rose.

Place small flowerpots on their side in your vegetable patch and you will often find snails resting inside. Destroy them at dusk (with a big boot on a path) and often slugs will feast on their remains – allowing you a second offensive. Hoe your vegetable patch thoroughly to disturb the soil: this brings eggs to the surface for thrushes, blackbirds and robins.

Protect your key plants with 'decoys': the best slug magnets are lettuces and African marigolds, both of which attract slugs at dusk. Collect and destroy them – wear rubber gloves if squeamish. Always harden off young plants to toughen the growth and avoid quick-release plant foods. These promote soft, sappy growth – a gourmet feast for gastropods.

SECRETS OF SUCCESS

- Certain plants attract slugs more than others. Protect vulnerable crops, like runner beans, with decoy plants and then collect the slugs off the decoy plants.
- Slugs prefer soft, leafy growth. Don't over-feed your plants with nitrogen (it will make them irresistible) and always harden them off for a week when they come out of the greenhouse or from a garden centre.
- Aromatic plants and silver-leaved plants are unpopular with slugs.

TYPES OF SLUG

Grey Field Slug (*Derocereas reticulatum*)
The most common and serious slug pest. Usually light grey or fawn and measuring 3cm (1½in), this is the very soft-bodied slug you find in lettuces and cabbages.

Keeled Slug (*Tandonia budapestensis*)
Grey-black with a ridge down the back. These are larger than the Grey Field slug (about 6–7cm/2½in) and they tend to live and feed underground. Potatoes are a delicacy to them.

Black Slug (*Arion ater*)
This is the large slug you are likely to see in the daytime after rain. It can measure up to 20cm (8in) and is black in colour, although some subspecies have a distinctive orange colour. This type cleans up debris – don't kill it. It feeds on rotting foliage, fungi and petals.

Garden Slug (*Arion hortensis*)
A slug with tough, leathery skin. Darker in colour (grey–black) with a paler, yellowish underside. Destructive at every level – and this one can climb.

Did you know? Not all slugs are bad for the garden. Many of the larger ones clean up plant debris under the ground, so they shouldn't be killed indiscriminately. The time to catch the real baddies is half an hour before dusk, when they are at their most active.

6 Sow Cucurbits
(late April)

CUCURBITS – cucumbers, courgettes, pumpkins and squashes – are the most frost-tender plants in the vegetable garden. You can sow them under glass now, but these plants should never go out into the garden until the first week of June. If you put them outside in May, be prepared to cover them at night. The slightest frost will turn them to mush and cold nights will check their growth so severely that they will never recover. They resent cool temperatures and wind bruises the leaves very easily.

Varieties differ a great deal. If you raise your own plants you can select good varieties suited to your needs. The seeds are large and oval and they can rot if laid flat on to compost. Place them vertically to avoid this problem, pushing them down about 1cm (½in). There is no reason to chip or soak seeds – they generally germinate well in warmth and light.

Place one seed in a 7.5cm (3in) pot almost full of seed compost. Label clearly, as cucurbits all look very similar when young. Water thoroughly, and then leave the pots until the seeds have germinated. It will take several weeks for a plant to develop to the planting-out stage and it's best to keep watering the pots every morning so that the seedlings sit in drier compost overnight. Fleece the young plants if a cold night is forecast.

These days the marrow has been usurped by the winter squash, which has to be stored for at least 6 weeks to develop its nutty, sweet flavour. There are excellent outdoor F1 hybrid cucumbers and many courgettes that produce small fruits that won't turn into marrows.

SECRETS OF SUCCESS

- Grow the plants to a good size under glass before planting out. Feed with liquid nitrogen-rich plant food if necessary.
- Fleece if a frost is forecast.
- Water well during summer and feed with chicken manure, which is available as a powder and as pellets. Ease off the watering in autumn.
- The grey-skinned 'Crown Prince' and 'Blue Hubbard' squashes keep the longest – often until late April. However, they are thin-skinned and more susceptible to frost damage once harvested.

Did you know? Pumpkin seeds have been found in burial caves in Mexico dating back to 8000 BC. Pumpkin is the food that sustained the Pilgrim Fathers and in October 1621 at the first Thanksgiving Day meal boiled pumpkin was served, but these days Americans prefer pumpkin pie instead.

VARIETIES

Courgette
'Romanesco' AGM
Long-cropping, this Italian variety produces slender, ridged courgettes with a nutty flavour.

Courgette
'Venus' F1
A compact courgette producing shiny, dark-green fruits. Could be grown in a container.

Cucumber
'Iznik' F1
A small cocktail cucumber for outdoors, producing up to 12.5cm (5in) long fruits with a good flavour. Could be grown in a container.

Cucumber
'Marketmore' AGM
The most prolific small cucumber for outdoor use. Spiny, tasty fruits and lots of them.

Winter Squash
'Sunshine'
A Japanese squash, round, orange and with a superb flavour. Each one weighs 2kg (4lb) and keeps until late January.

Winter Squash
'Uchiki Kuri'
The Japanese red onion squash, which is almost pear-shaped. The flavour is excellent and this also keeps until late January. 2.5kg (5lb).

Organic Tip ✔

Once your cucurbits go outside, cloche them at night using rigid plastic or glass bell cloches. This will double their size and produce an earlier crop, because they need warmth to photosynthesize.

MAY

May is a glorious month, the transition between spring and summer, and much of the hard work in the vegetable garden has already been completed. Most hardy crops are in the ground and, we hope, racing away and full of promise. You can almost hear things growing – but, sadly, that includes the weeds too. The hoe is the finest implement ever created. Use it every week between rows to get rid of weed seedlings. It will disrupt the enemy too – slugs hate disturbance. Hoeing also aerates the top layer of soil, helping rain to penetrate, but its usefulness doesn't end there. The fine dust you create acts as a mulch and helps to keep moisture in the soil.

A word or two of caution: this is the time of the year when the difference between nighttime and daytime temperatures can be at its greatest. These see-sawing temperatures create poor growing conditions, especially for frost-tender plants. Don't be in a hurry to put any tender crops outside until late May. Better still, wait for early June!

1 Plant Tomatoes under Glass

(*early May*)

IF YOU have an unheated greenhouse it's time to put in your tomato plants. There will be plenty on offer in garden centres. Look for good-sized plants that have green foliage. If the foliage looks even slightly blackened, don't buy them: these plants have suffered a cold shock and it is likely to hamper them permanently.

Some varieties are best trained as cordons, others left to grow as a bush, and some have a trailing habit. Varieties are therefore classed as one of these forms: cordons, bushes and trailing. Cordons are easier to manage because they take up less space, but they do need staking securely. The side shoots are pinched out to create an upright plant and fruiting trusses are limited to six. Bush varieties and trailing (or tumbling) varieties are allowed to develop naturally. Their habit varies, but some sprawl and take up a lot of ground room. They are suited to growbags and containers. Fruit varies in shape from plum to cherry, from beefsteak to the more conventional round fruit. There are reds, oranges and yellows too, although I have yet to find a yellow variety with a good flavour.

Recently, grafted tomatoes (which have been used by commercial growers for decades) have become available to the home gardener too. These have the advantage of being guaranteed to be free of soil-borne disease. They are grafted on to vigorous rootstocks and this makes them grow far more quickly and aggressively. Be prepared to remove some of the leaves if necessary so that the fruit is exposed to the sun. They can make huge plants that threaten to take over your greenhouse. The ones I have tried ripened poorly when grown outdoors.

Did you know? Tomatoes belong to the Solanum family (just like potatoes) and they also suffer from potato blight, so don't grow the two close together. Both come from Peru, but wild tomatoes thrive in the warm, damp lowlands that separate the Andes from the Pacific while the potato is a high-altitude plant.

SECRETS OF SUCCESS

- Try to keep the temperature as level as possible. Make sure that the greenhouse is shut up well before dusk and that it is ventilated during the day. Ideally, temperatures should be between 20°C and 24°C (68° and 75°F).
- Plant in fertile soil, and stake and support immediately.
- Water in well when you plant, then stand back for a few days to encourage the roots to search for water.
- Once you see the plants beginning to grow, water them again. Stick to a regular watering regime: uneven watering causes the tomatoes to split. Try to water in the morning if possible.
- Pinch out the side shoots of cordons with your fingers. They appear in the axil between stem and leaf. Wear gloves if you have sensitive skin.
- Once the first truss of flowers is set, water on a high-potash commercial tomato food or diluted comfrey tea (see page 69) every 14 days.

Organic Tip ✔

Tear off tattered foliage, etc., rather than cutting it. Commercial growers adopt this approach as it prevents disease entering the plant.

2 Sprinkle Orange Annuals
(early May)

VEGETABLE gardeners need their pollinators and bees are obviously vital. Hoverflies also pollinate and their almost transparent larvae pre-date aphids and other small creatures, providing pollination and pest control. Adult hoverflies lay their eggs near aphid colonies and then their maggot-like larvae feed on them.

Hoverflies need nectar for flight and pollen for breeding, but they have tiny mouths and therefore prefer tiny flowers. Umbellifers are highly attractive to them. The green-flowered *Bupleurum griffithii* 'Decor' is an easily grown annual and it will self-seed once established. *Ammi majus*, *A. visnaga* and *Orlaya grandiflora* are three other umbellifers with white flowers that could also be used. These need to be sown in trays and planted outside.

Hoverflies are also strongly attracted to bright orange and yellow, and the orange pot marigold (*Calendula officinalis*) will lure them in. This is one of the easiest annuals to grow. Simply sprinkle the crescent-shaped seeds on to damp ground and lightly cover them with soil or compost. Let them grow to flowering size, then dead-head them until late summer. After that they can be allowed to self-seed. French marigolds (*Tagetes patula*) are also excellent and plants should still be available at garden centres. Avoid the double forms: they are less insect friendly.

SECRETS OF SUCCESS

- Grow a range of annuals that flower between midsummer and late autumn. Try to avoid fully double-flowered forms, because the extra petals replace the stamens and other flower parts. Insects cannot access the flowers and, even if they could, there is rarely any pollen or nectar.
- Choose hardy, easy annuals that can be sown directly into the soil.
- Choose a warm, damp day and rake over the soil, sprinkle on the seeds and add a light covering of compost or soil.
- Dead-head regularly to prevent seeds forming until late August, then allow some plants to set seed.
- Save your own seeds. Collect them on dry days and packet them up. A biscuit tin in the fridge is ideal for storage.

Did you know? The Marmalade hoverfly is very common in gardens. It is one of 276 species of hoverfly in Britain. Its orange body has double black stripes. One larva will eat several hundred aphids during its 14-day lifespan.

VARIETIES

Cornflower
Centaurea cyanus
The blue cornflower is one of the few true blues of summer. Sown now, it is usually in flower by midsummer. This is the preferred annual flower of the red-tailed bumble bee, but hoverflies also visit.

Cosmos
Cosmos bipinnatus 'Antiquity'
A shorter cosmos in a mix of pinks. This simple saucer flowers from late June until late into the year if you dead-head. Popular with bees and hoverflies.

Pot Marigold
Calendula officinalis 'Indian Prince'
A classy, maroon-centred, single orange pot marigold. It is so much more rewarding for insects than the very full doubles often sold.

Scabious
Scabiosa atropurpurea
This will supply a succession of pincushion scabious throughout summer and autumn. Rich maroons, whites and Beaujolais mixes are all on offer and the insects seem to like them all.

Organic Tip ✔

Try to plant your annuals in a warm position, preferably where afternoon sun falls, because nectar always flows more freely in warmer temperatures. Leave flowering annuals in the ground as late into the year as possible for foraging bees.

3 Feed Your Plants with Comfrey Tea

(mid-May)

YOUR SUMMER bedding plants and vegetables in containers are probably growing in commercial compost which will sustain them for only 6 weeks at most. So now is the perfect time to start watering on a fortnightly liquid feed to boost flowers and fruit.

Choose your water-on plant food wisely. Some nitrogen-rich feeds only promote leafy growth. These are ideal for boosting young yew hedges, cabbages and container-grown topiary, but for flowers and fruit you need to use a potash-rich liquid tomato food.

You can make your own high-potash food for free using comfrey leaves. Comfrey is a member of the borage family and 'Bocking 14' is the best clone. Put the chopped leaves in a container with a lid and leave them to rot for a couple of weeks. No water is required. As the leaves decompose they produce a brown liquid called comfrey tea. This can be diluted one part comfrey tea to twenty parts water.

The liquid can smell, but Garden Organic at Ryton produce a wall-mounted drainpipe system that saves you opening the lid. The pipe has removable lids on both ends. The leaves go in the top and, once rotted, the liquid is drained from the bottom.

Chopped comfrey leaves can also be used as an accelerator on the compost heap to speed up decomposition. Just make a layer of leaves on the top. Plant three or four plants of 'Bocking 14' by your compost heap so that it's handy.

Did you know? The benefits of growing comfrey were discovered by Henry Doubleday (1810–1902). He wanted to patent a glue for postage stamps and he imported comfrey from Russia with the aim of extracting glue from the mucilaginous roots. He discovered that comfrey stayed in leaf for 10 months of the year and wrote about his findings in the *Gardener's Chronicle and Agricultural Gazette*. Years later, the famous organic gardener Lawrence Hills (1911–91) discovered the articles and visited Bocking, the village near Braintree in Essex where Henry Doubleday had lived. He found Henry's descendants (nonagenarians Edith and Thomas) in residence – still growing comfrey. Lawrence Hills identified a strain which he called 'Bocking 14' as the best. Its leaves contain twice as much potash as ordinary comfrey.

COMFREYS

Symphytum uplandicum **'Bocking 14'**
Originally imported from Russia, this kitchen-garden clone is available from organic gardening catalogues.

Symphytum caucasicum
This pretty comfrey is tall and elegant with sky-blue flowers and soft-green leaves. It is adored by bees, so makes a good addition in a wilder area of the plot.

Organic Tip ✔

Comfrey leaves should always be placed at the bottom of the potato trench because as they decompose they release nutrients that boost your crop.

- Comfrey produces nectar-rich flowers in May, just when other flowers are in short supply. Pulmonarias are in the same family and they too flower well in spring. Both are popular with bees. However, when you grow 'Bocking 14' for tea, don't let it flower.
- After flowering, cut the leaves from the base to leave a stump. Chop the leaves and stems up roughly and make the first batch of comfrey tea. Repeat the process throughout summer. You should be able to get at least four cuts.
- The ratio of nutrients in 'Bocking 14' is almost the same as in commercial tomato foods. Comfrey tea should be used every 2 weeks to promote flowers and fruit in the vegetable and flower garden. It will save you the expense of buying commercial tomato feed.
- Once you've planted comfrey, it's difficult to dig up. Always place the plants carefully and avoid any smothering groundcover varieties such as *Symphytum grandiflorum*. Remove the flowering stems as they fade.
- 'Bocking 14' is sterile, but other types self-seed prolifically.

4 Sow Runner and French Beans Outdoors

(*mid-May*)

IT'S TIME to sow frost-tender runner beans and French beans straight into the ground, because the soil is now warm enough to ensure rapid germination. Always put the poles up before sowing any climbing varieties. I find a wigwam of eight tall canes (securely tied at the top) withstands strong winds much better than a long row. Beans have soft leaves and they suffer horribly in strong winds. Sow three beans round each cane and thin if necessary once they come up. Also sow a handful in the middle of the tripod or at the end of the row for filling in gaps.

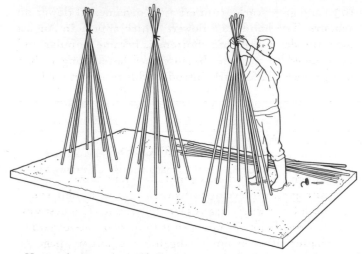

Keep slugs at bay. If they nip out the growing points the beans will not recover. Adding lettuces to the area helps to lure them away from the beans.

Try to sow at least two varieties of runner bean because they are influenced by the weather. White-flowered runner beans have paler seeds and red-flowered forms have darker seeds. As a general rule, the paler the seed the more heat-tolerant the variety is. Red-flowered beans often drop their flowers in hot weather once the nighttime temperature reaches 16°C (62°F). White-flowered varieties thrive in warmer summers.

Climbing French beans also prefer hot summers and the dark-podded 'Blauhilde' and the green 'Cobra' are star performers. Flat-podded varieties (like 'Pantheon' and 'Hunter') crop very heavily whatever the weather. Growing a selection of varieties will ensure a crop no matter what summer brings. New hybrid varieties with both French and runner-bean blood are available.

Did you know? The runner bean was grown as an ornamental plant when it was first introduced in 1633 by John Tradescant the Elder. He became gardener to Charles I in 1630 and grew scarlet runners as an ornamental flower on arbours. The handsome flowers, which appear in August once the day length has shortened, became popular and were added to nosegays because they lasted longer than many others. These early introductions rarely set seed.

SECRETS OF SUCCESS

- Although beans and peas generally resent extra nitrogen, preferring to fix their own with their root nodules, runner beans seem to need it. The best way to provide lots of nitrogen is to incorporate organic matter either by double digging (see January, page 7) or by making a bean trench (see January, page 16)
- Bide your time: don't expose runner beans to nighttime temperatures until early June.
- Sow at least two varieties – one white-flowered and one red, because white-flowered varieties are more heat-tolerant than red ones.
- Find a sheltered position out of the wind. If your garden is windy, plant wigwams, not rows. They resist the force of the wind much better. Water the beans well until they get to the top of the canes.
- Once they begin to flower, water them if the weather is dry.
- Once they reach the top of the pole, pinch out the shoots so that they bush out lower down.
- Sow a second lot in June for an autumn crop.
- Pick your crop regularly. Often August is a peak month, so if you plan to go on holiday then recruit a neighbour to pick them and eat them for you.

VARIETIES

'Polestar'
Probably the finest red-flowered string-less runner-bean variety, producing a long succession of thick, fleshy pods until late in the season. Lots of fleshy, tender, smooth-skinned beans.

'Red Rum' AGM
The earliest red-flowered runner bean to crop, producing medium-length, string-less, straight pods. This variety is often over by August, so do grow a late variety too.

'White Emergo'
A white-flowered runner bean producing very smooth, light-green pods.

'Moonlight'
The first runner x French hybrid. Vigorous and long-cropping, producing pods that resemble the runner bean in shape, but when snapped the pods have the plumper profile of a French bean.

'Lady Di'
Red-flowered, stringless runner bean with long, straight pods.

'Wisley Magic'
Very prolific and capable of doing well in hot weather, with a good runner-bean flavour.

Organic Tip ✔

Only sow in the middle of May if you feel we are poised on the edge of summer. If mid–May is cold, wait for the weather.

5 Re-sow Early Crops
(late May)

MANY OF the crops you sowed a few weeks ago will be racing away, but if you have room, sow another batch now. They will crop in the autumn and extend your productive season. You will need to water these new rows, as we should be entering the driest, hottest time of the year.

Re-sow three types of lettuce but make sure that one is a Cos: these are slower to bolt than the others. Bolting is normally a lot less likely after Midsummer's Day (21 June), but exceptionally dry summers can still send every lettuce into seed. Your sowings of beetroot can also be repeated, using the same varieties.

Your earliest sowing of carrots included fast-maturing varieties like 'Amsterdam Forcing 3' and 'Nantes Early 2'. Now it's time to change to slower-maturing varieties capable of staying in the ground into autumn and beyond. The following three AGM varieties are all F1 hybrids: 'Bangor', 'Eskimo' and 'Kingston'. Once mature, they will all stand low temperatures. However, if you continue sowing up until mid-August, it's best to switch back to faster-maturing varieties again as these crop more quickly.

Peas can be succession-sown every 2 weeks. The head gardeners managing large walled gardens devoted more room to them than to any other crop for that reason. Peas can be sown up until the middle of July and still crop. In fact, these cool-season crops do well from July sowings. Alongside the varieties listed overleaf, 'Hurst Greenshaft' does well sown late.

SECRETS OF SUCCESS

- Sowing in May provides autumn crops, but watering is more important for these sowings because hot, dry weather often arrives in June just as they are starting into growth. Morning watering is the most efficient.
- If you're sowing any crop in late July, opt for a fast-maturing variety, particularly for root crops.
- Peas enjoy cool weather and can tolerate some shade.
- Pinch out growing tips on later-sown peas and beans as soon as the first pods are ready at the bottom of the plants.

> **Did you know?** Early pea varieties were not very sweet until the Herefordshire cider-maker Thomas Knight started to hybridize peas in the nineteenth century. He used his experience as a cider-apple-grower, selecting and crossing for sweetness, and created wrinkle-seeded peas that could be eaten raw. From 1811 to 1838 Knight was one of the first presidents of what eventually became the Royal Horticultural Society.

VARIETIES FOR SUCCESSION SOWING

Carrot
'Eskimo' AGM
The most cold-tolerant variety, it can be overwintered on well-drained soils. A very strong variety with robust tops. Crown normally below soil level.

Pea
'Dorian' AGM
The long, broad, straight pods contain eight to ten large, tasty peas and this variety was once known as 'Mr Big'. A good crop of pods for picking over a long period.

Pea
'Balmoral' AGM
The ideal pea for a May–June sowing with an autumn harvest in mind. Seven sweet peas in each pod. Dark, handsome foliage and a good yield.

Pea
'Kelvedon Wonder' AGM
This 1925 stalwart variety is still considered the best for regular successional sowings. Heavy crops of narrow, pointed pods in pairs, averaging seven or eight succulent peas per pod. Excellent from a June sowing.

Organic Tip ✔

Be adventurous: push back the boundaries and experiment with late-sown crops because autumns are tending to be warmer and more frost-free than they were.

6 Sow Witloof Chicory
(late May)

THERE ARE lots of different varieties of chicory, including red-leaved and curly forms called radicchio. Witloof chicory is a special type suitable for forcing as a winter vegetable. You must choose Witloof if you want to produce the pale, pointed chicons (as the blanched chicory heads are called). These resemble small Cos lettuces and can be eaten in the darkest days of winter when many other crops may be frozen into the ground. Eaten fresh and shredded into a salad, Witloof has a bittersweet, crunchy texture. When cooked, its bitter flavour balances creamy chicken dishes.

When the crop is in the ground, Witloof chicory looks like oversized dandelions and the tops stay green during winter. It can be sown now, ready to be planted outside in late June or early July. You can sow it outside in a row and then thin, but the plants have to be spaced 30cm (12in) apart, so raising them in pots is easier. Sow seeds in a seed tray, then prick them out individually in small plastic pots. Twenty-five plants would probably be enough for most gardeners. The plants are lifted from November onwards for forcing (see page 169).

VARIETIES

'Witloof Zoom' F1
Go for this F1 hybrid every time because it has the vigour to produce a plump, pale chicon in 4 weeks.

'Variegata del Castelfranco'
This is the hardiest chicory of all. It can be grown and eaten in leaf, or left to heart up, or it can be forced.

'Treviso Rosso'
A red-leaved chicory that can be eaten as a leaf during winter. It can also be lifted and forced.

SECRETS OF SUCCESS

- Seeds can be sown straight into the open ground and then thinned out so that each rosette is 30cm (12in) apart.
- Sowing in pots is easier, but these tap-rooted plants must be transplanted young.
- Keep the plants weed-free and water well in dry conditions.
- You can either select and lift plants as and when you need them from early November onwards, or you can lift all the roots at once, storing them horizontally in peat or sand in a box in a cool shed or garage.
- Force a few of the roots at a time. Up to five roots will fit into a 22cm (9in) flowerpot. This is a convenient size to cover with a bucket. If you use an upturned flowerpot, cover the holes to exclude any light.
- Choose a dark place that's not too warm for forcing – 16–18°C (61–64°F) is ideal.
- Keep the pot of compost or soil moist and warm. Your chicons will be ready to harvest in about 3–4 weeks. Lift a little sooner if you want smaller ones.

Did you know? Witloof Chicory was discovered in 1830 by accident by a Belgian farmer who was growing chicory roots. These were used as a cheap coffee substitute. While storing roots in his cellar, he noticed the new white leaves, tasted them and found them moist, crunchy and slightly bitter.

Organic Tip ✔

*Dark conditions are essential for forcing chicory and the flavour is better.
Too much light causes the leaves to become over-bitter.*

SUMMER TASKS

To Do

Thin crops as needed

Concentrate on watering in the first half of summer

Feed tomatoes, peppers, chillies and aubergines with potash-rich food every 2 weeks

Weed assiduously – a hoe is the most useful tool now

Cloche young cucurbits at night in June

Stop picking asparagus

Cut back herbs to encourage fresh growth

Apply mulch in dry summers

Be vigilant about Cabbage White butterflies and asparagus

Look out for potato blight. Cut away and bin infected leaves

Harvest regularly

Loosen onions and shallots, then lift, dry and store

Check tomatoes – the yield of fruit is at its highest in August

Sow Outdoors

Continue to repeat-sow all outdoor hardy crops

Runner and French beans

Florence fennel

Swiss chard

Japanese onions (August)

Short-term green manures (August)

Sow under Glass

Summer and autumn
    cauliflowers
Chicory for forcing
Cabbages – red, summer,
    autumn and winter varieties
    (June–July)
Spring cabbages (August)

Plant

Tomatoes – outdoor and indoor
Peppers
Aubergines
All cucurbits – cucumber,
    squash, pumpkin, courgette,
    etc.
Sweetcorn – in a block
Leeks
Winter brassicas – Brussels
    sprouts, kale, cabbage,
    purple sprouting broccoli

JUNE

*J*une can be the softest month of all and those long summer evenings
should give you a chance to relax now that much of the hard
work is done.

Keep up the hoeing, weeding and watering – especially the
watering. If you neglect that in June, your yields will suffer – even
if it pours in July. We are still in a growth spurt. Up until the
longest day, most crops are raring to go; after that they slow down.
I have learned this the hard way.

Although June is the start of the summer season, there's often a
hungry gap. Lots of crops sown or planted in spring won't deliver
until the end of the month at the earliest. But don't despair – soon
you'll be harvesting baby potatoes, scrumping peas and wondering
how you are going to manage to harvest it all.

1 Watering
(early June)

WATERING the right way at the right time is an art. It's one of the keys to preventing certain crops from bolting, but lack of water is only part of the reason for vegetables running to seed. A lot of crops get stressed by cold spring winds and cold nighttime temperatures – something over which we have little influence, although fleecing can help. The best way round these last two problems is to plant later. Every region of Britain has a slightly different optimum time and it can vary within a few miles.

Watering is something most inexperienced gardeners get wrong indoors and out. Seedlings hate being wet and cold, so if you are going to water them, try to get it over with by 4 p.m. Then they have chance to recover and dry off before both enemies arrive on the scenes – the slug and cold nighttime temperatures. Invest in a good watering can with a fine rose. Point the rose up for seedlings (to emulate fine rain) and point it downwards to drench larger plants. If seedlings and young plants get too wet, they won't develop a good root system because the roots won't have to search out water.

Don't dribble the hose or can over your garden crops – that only makes the roots come to the surface and they should be heading downwards. Drench your plot for at least 3 hours with a sprinkler or a seep hose. This can be done overnight on warm nights. Three to four bouts of watering are ideal, but even one long watering session will deliver. Always use water wisely and only water if it's vital.

Did you know? The Aztecs used a plant they called *accotli* (literally 'hollow pipe') to water their crops. This tall plant grew to 10m (30ft) tall and the stems were felled to make pipes to take water to the crops. In 1789 specimens of *accotli* were collected and sent to the Royal Gardens in Madrid, where the curator, l'Abbé Cavanilles, named the flowers after his Swedish horticultural assistant, Andreas Dahl. The dahlia had arrived in Europe.

SECRETS OF SUCCESS

- Set up an irrigation system in early spring if you have well-drained soil. Use a timer if necessary. Remove it in autumn.
- Seep hoses deliver a slow drip from their sides. They work well as long as there are no kinks or sharp bends in them.
- Porous hoses can be snaked around your plot, as they exude water from all round their circumference. They can be buried to a depth of 10cm (4in).
- Sprinklers are adaptable because you can move them, but avoid using them for certain crops. Some (such as potatoes) are prone to disease if their foliage gets wet.
- Have water butts, as many as you can place, but use this water only on larger plants. It can encourage damping off (a fungal disease) if used on seedlings.
- Tapwater is best for seedlings because it is more or less sterile. It should stand in a can for several hours to warm up. This will also allow some of the chlorine from mains water to escape. Every time you empty a can, fill it up again.

Organic Tip ✔

Mulching helps enormously with water conservation. Grass clippings can be used round large plants like globe artichokes. However, they need to be partially rotted. Lay them on a sheet in the sun until they brown. Turn them once and then apply as a mulch — always on damp soil.

GUIDE TO WATERING

Watering near dusk encourages slugs.

Onions, garlic and shallots have short, stumpy roots that cannot search for water. If these crops become dry early in the year they don't develop.

Beetroot needs water from late spring into summer.

Newly planted leeks are puddled in (see page 19) and this helps initially. One good watering after that helps enormously.

All the cucurbits (squashes, courgettes, cucumbers and pumpkins) love warm, moist conditions and, if the weather fails them, you will need to provide water.

Carrots and parsnips are less fussy — their tap roots help them out.

Potatoes can tolerate drought, although the yield will be smaller.

2 Plant Outdoor Tomatoes

(early June)

THE BEST flavour of all comes from the outdoor-grown tomato, but the British climate is not always warm enough to encourage lots of fruit on traditional tomato varieties. These are often warm-weather plants more suited to being grown under glass. However, in recent years the seed industry has tapped into cold-tolerant varieties from

Russia and eastern Europe. These can perform outdoors, although an outdoor tomato is likely to produce around half the fruit you could expect from an indoor one. Generally a crop of four trusses is a good result.

The main problem with growing outdoor tomatoes is their susceptibility to potato blight (*Phytophthora infestans*). This generally appears in August, just when outdoor tomatoes are at their peak, and it usually stops them in their tracks – they just wither and die. Luckily, some of the eastern European varieties are proving very blight-resistant and it is these that gardeners should be seeking out.

Outdoor varieties tend to be bushy and are often best left to develop naturally. The tomatoes are often smaller, but tasty. Plants can be grown in growbags or in pots. I prefer pots: they are easier to move. Plants in south-facing positions against buildings sometimes need moving in summer heatwaves. If you have a very warm position, plant them in the ground.

There are also hanging-basket varieties, but I would grow these in pots too. They are easier to water and they are portable.

Did you know? Until the end of the nineteenth century the tomato was regarded as highly suspicious and possibly poisonous, probably because the flowers resembled those of the notoriously poisonous deadly nightshade, However, cheap glass, which became available in the late 1860s, fuelled their popularity and huge greenhouses were constructed in the Lea Valley in London and along the south coast. A quarter of the tomatoes we eat today are British-grown. Many come from the Isle of Wight – arguably the sunniest place in Britain.

SECRETS OF SUCCESS

- Choose blight-resistant varieties if possible — those with flavour.
- Offer your tomatoes sun and shelter, but don't plant them outside until June.
- Strong plants throw off infection. Water regularly and feed as soon as the first fruit is set, using a liquid tomato food or comfrey tea (see page 69) every 2 weeks.
- Fleece in September if a frost is forecast.

BLIGHT-RESISTANT OUTDOOR VARIETIES

'Stupice'
This cordon variety will need the side shoots pinching out. An early-ripening, cold-tolerant, 'potato-leaved' variety from the Czech Republic. Produces clusters of golf-ball-sized red fruit with a good flavour. A heavy cropper that's ideal for growing outdoors.

'Legend' AGM
This American-bred bush variety has shown great blight resistance in the garden. Produces a heavy crop of large, glossy red fruits.

'Koralik'
This heritage Russian bush variety crops before the main August wave of blight, although it has shown good tolerance to blight in 3 years of trials. The small, bright-red tomatoes on each truss ripen together.

'Premio' F1
This extensively trialled cordon variety produces handsome red fruit with shiny red skin. It ripens well and evenly, and the taste is outstanding.

'Losetto'
A cascading bush variety with exceptional blight resistance that's ideal for hanging baskets, containers or a sunny spot in the garden. Cherry-sized, sweet-tasting, round red fruits.

'Fantasio' F1
A prolific cropper bearing medium-sized red fruit. Vigorous, with healthy green foliage — leave it to its own devices. Grow as a cordon.

3 Sow Squashes and Pumpkins Outdoors

(mid-June)

AT THIS time of year it's possible to sow courgette, squash and pumpkin seeds straight into the sun-warmed ground, into a large pot or a growbag. This later planting will soon catch up with the transplanted spring-sown cucurbits and, having been sown now that the nights are warmer, your plants will race away.

The most useful crop of the three is the winter squash. The fruits are cut, ripened outside and then stored for several weeks before being eaten. This resting period in cooler weather allows the starch to turn to sugar. If you are still growing the tasteless marrow, replace it with winter squash immediately!

Squashes need space: they creep over the ground and for that reason they make a good follow-up act after first early potatoes. As they expand they cover the gaps where you've harvested. Potatoes are hungry feeders and their thick foliage tends to exclude rain, so you must enrich the ground before planting squash. Water it thoroughly or wait for rain. Sprinkle on blood, fish and bone (see page 158) and then make a mound 30cm (1ft) high and 60cm (2ft) wide. Space two squash seeds along the mound and then let them fight it out. Pumpkins can be treated in the same way. Alternatively, you can plant some seeds or add a couple of young plants into the top of a well-rotted compost heap – the warmth beneath will give them a boost. If space is tight, sow one or two courgettes instead.

Did you know? One of the most historic squashes is the enormous, teardrop-shaped 'Blue Hubbard'. It was grown in the Americas by native tribes and then by settlers and probably arrived in the USA in the 1700s aboard sailing ships coming from the West Indies. In 1842 a woman named Elizabeth Hubbard mentioned the squash to her neighbour, a seed-trader named James Gregory, who then introduced it as the 'Hubbard' squash.

SECRETS OF SUCCESS

- Warmth, water and fertile soil are essential requirements.
- The large leaves of cucurbits tend to cover the ground and keep moisture in, although you may want to mulch early on.
- Only harvest ripe fruits – the fruit stems should feel woody and corky.
- When cutting, leave a length of stem, then store the fruits upside down on a slatted seat or bench so that they harden and ripen in the sun.
- Grey-skinned squashes store until late April, so use the orange and butternut squashes first.
- Cook squashes from mid-November onwards. Cut them up, then remove and discard the pips. Dice the flesh into 5cm (2in) cubes, adding herbs and oil before roasting.

Organic Tip ✔

Always store squashes and pumpkins stem down because moisture can collect in the hollow round the stem, which can lead to rotting. They keep for much longer upside down.

4 Plant Cucumbers
(mid-June)

IF YOU'RE growing lettuce and tomatoes you should aspire to cucumbers too. Outdoor varieties can be trained up and over a compost heap, or fitted into small niches in the vegetable garden – somewhere sheltered that can accommodate a simple 1m (3ft) high trellis. It's still possible to sow F1 seeds (see page 39) but ready-grown plants should also
be available now.

Outdoor cucumbers are short and rotund, often with spiny skins. Normally they measure only about 15cm (6in) in length, but picked young they have a lovely nutty flavour and their compact size means that one can be consumed easily in a sitting. Given plenty of water, it's possible to harvest one every other day in the second half of summer – so they are well worth growing. Cucumbers prefer cool, moist air (ideally with temperatures around 20°C (70°F)) and it's often possible to tuck one plant of an indoor variety at the back of a greenhouse where tomatoes are being grown. Indoor varieties produce long, straight fruits similar to those in supermarkets. Of the two, I prefer the outdoor ones, thinly sliced in wafer-thin white bread on a perfect summer's day.

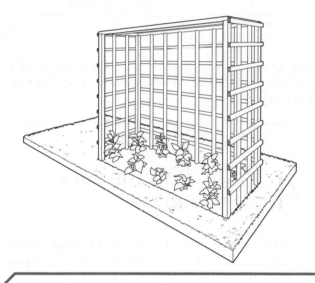

Organic Tip ✔

Don't allow your cucumbers to become old and develop thick, bitter skins. They are more beneficial eaten with their skins on, as all the antioxidants are contained in the dark skin.

SECRETS OF SUCCESS

- All cucumbers are soft-leaved and therefore resent windy conditions. Find them somewhere sheltered, ideally where afternoon sun falls. Midday sun is too much for them.
- Avoid cold nights. Fleece or cover with cloches on cool June nights.
- F1 cucumber seeds are eye-wateringly expensive. When sowing, insert them into compost vertically with the sharp end down to lessen the chance of them rotting in the compost.
- Grow self-fertile all-female varieties under glass. These never produce bitter fruits and you don't have to pick off the male flowers. Never, ever pick off the male flowers on outdoor varieties: they are needed for cross-pollination.
- Sow up until mid-June in small round pots (placing one seed in each) or create a fertile mound and sow into it (see page 88).
- Support with canes and string. Water in well before evening descends, as slugs target cucumbers. Train upwards — away from the ground.
- Feed every 2 weeks with liquid tomato food or home-made comfrey tea (see page 69).
- Water little and often. Stressed cucumbers succumb to mildew, but don't panic if this happens. Ignore it.
- Cucumbers need lots of water, but their stems can rot in wet soil. Sinking a flowerpot into the ground a little distance from the main stem and watering into that works well.

> **Did you know?** The Roman Emperor Tiberius (42 BC–AD 37) had a passion for cucumbers and his gardeners strove to grow them all year long using portable cold frames. Henry VIII felt just the same, and Columbus even took seeds to the New World. The Victorians grew them widely — and the straight cucumber was desirable even then. Long glass jars were used to stop the fruit from curving.

VARIETIES

'Tiffany' F1 AGM
An all-female, vigorous F1 hybrid for the greenhouse, producing lots of dark-skinned 30cm (12in) long fruits . Good powdery mildew resistance.

'Carmen' F1 Hybrid
An all-female, very disease-resistant variety that crops abundantly, producing over fifty fruits in a season. Easy to train and day-length sensitive, which means most flowers are produced when there are 11 hours of day length. Sow after 1 March.

'Masterpiece' AGM
Short, straight outdoor cucumber with tasty, dark-green fruits about 20cm (8in) in length.

'Marketmore' AGM
Stalwart outdoor variety, producing a good yield of dark-green fruits. A consistent, disease-resistant cucumber.

For further varieties, see April, page 62.

5 Stop Harvesting Asparagus
(late June)

FOR NOTES on planting and cutting asparagus, see page 145. The asparagus season ends on Midsummer's Day or thereabouts, and cutting should now stop to allow the plants to regenerate for next year's crop. This shallow-rooted crop cannot be hoed very easily, so hand-weed the bed and lightly sprinkle blood, fish and bone round each plant. Do not overfeed asparagus, however. Watch out for female plants that produce seeds (these look like small berries) and remove any you see to prevent inferior seedlings popping up. Most modern varieties are all-male, so in theory it shouldn't happen. Stake any over-tall stems to stop them flopping.

Keep an eye out for asparagus beetles: they look a bit like elongated ladybirds, with orange, black and white bodies. Pick any off and destroy them, and check regularly for more. Leave the top growth intact at the moment, but cut it down when the foliage starts to fade to 2.5cm (1in) above the ground. This treatment will give your crop 4 or 5 months to recover for next year.

Asparagus is very long-lived and it can tie up the same plot of ground for decades. You need thirty crowns to stand any chance of a harvestable crop, so it isn't an option for small gardens – particularly when you realize it generally has only a 6-week season. However, if you have a large enough plot and you love it, grow it. It arrives in the hungriest moment of the gardening year, when most crops are getting established, and that's why country-house gardens still grow so much of it.

Did you know? Asparagus produces rather phallic spears and the Greek *spargao* (meaning 'turgid') reflected their tumescent shape. The sandy land close to Venice produced masses of white asparagus in the sixteenth century. When the Huguenots fled from France in 1685 they brought it with them and planted fields of it. Battersea asparagus was rated the best and the earliest, and 260 acres were devoted to the crop close to the river Thames.

SECRETS OF SUCCESS

- Plant asparagus only if you have room for thirty crowns. Otherwise you will never get a decent-sized crop.
- This crop requires great patience. You have to stand back and allow at least 3 years before you start cutting any spears — longer if you are raising plants from seed.
- Asparagus thrives in warm places on well-drained, fertile soil, so river banks with sandy, alluvial soil are perfect. Many gardeners on heavier land compensate by making a raised mound containing coarse grit and organic matter to provide adequate drainage.
- Plant new crowns in April on well-prepared, enriched and weed-free soil. Soak them for an hour or two first (if they look dry), then spread out the roots to form a wagonwheel shape. Space each crown 30cm (1ft) in rows over 1m (3ft) apart to a depth of 10cm (4in).
- Avoid planting in frost pockets.
- Try to pick every other day, but crops depend on warm weather.
- Always feed in March and avoid mulching. Asparagus is shallow-rooted and resents being mulched in spring.
- Mulch after cutting has stopped (in mid-June) and again in autumn. A 5cm (2in) layer is enough.

Organic Tip ✔

If you've suffered from asparagus beetle, don't add the stems to your compost heap — bin them. The newly hatched beetles overwinter in debris and the compost heap is a perfect place to shelter before emerging in the spring. In May and June the grey eggs are laid haphazardly along the stems and can be rubbed off easily with your finger.

6 Plant Aubergines
(late June)

AUBERGINES are a demanding crop to grow in the average British summer, but you can encourage them to produce a reasonable crop in containers placed in a sunny position. Use a rich, loam-based compost – John Innes No. 3 is perfect for vegetables – and find a bucket-sized container. Black plastic (which tends to absorb the heat) is fine.

You can also grow aubergines in the ground under cover, either in a greenhouse or a polytunnel. This system will give you at least twice as many aubergines as a container-grown plant. Aubergines seem to have challenged gardeners for centuries. The Moors used to force them successfully using hotbeds over 1,000 years ago. The heat was provided by decomposing manure – a technique also used to raise pineapples in Britain in the mid-nineteenth century.

You can make a simple hotbed by excavating a deep trench and filling it with organic matter, or animal manure. This will decompose and, as it does so, will warm up the soil. If you can get some overhead cover, this will trap any heat and create a hothouse effect. So excavating a bed in the greenhouse or polytunnel will work well.

However, you can also cover your hotbed with a cold frame. The temperature in the frame is on average 10°C (50°F) hotter than the outdoor temperature, and the difference between daytime and night-time temperatures is much closer too. With this arrangement your aubergines can go on to the covered hotbed in April and be up to 120cm (4ft) tall by June.

SECRETS OF SUCCESS

- Choose an early F1 variety — the ones that produce big, round fruit are the best. The cylindrical fruits do not cook as well: they turn grey.
- Warmth, water and a sheltered position are the key ingredients for this tomato relative. Try to provide all three.
- Feed with a weekly dose of liquid plant food, either tomato feed or home-made comfrey tea (see page 69).
- Keep well watered. Protect from slugs and snails, which will eat the young fruits. Slug hunts at dusk are a must.
- Pick the fruit regularly, even if it's small.
- Dry air means your aubergines will almost certainly fall victim to spider mite. Spray regularly with water or use a biocontrol.

Organic Tip ✔

Ensure the ground is moist around your plants to keep down red mites. Aphids can also be a problem — but allow your predators to deal with them.

VARIETIES

'Bonica' F1 AGM
Glossy, black fruits early in the season on a tall, vigorous plant. Best in the ground.

'Fairy Tale' AGM
A new compact variety with egg-shaped fruits in purple and white. Good on a sunny patio.

'Black Enorma' F1
Huge, egg-shaped, dark fruits. Very prolific and carries on cropping late.

'Bellezza Nera'
Beautiful, fluted, wide fruits that cook equally beautifully. Very large and dusky purple rather than black. Not the same as 'Black Beauty'.

Did you know? During the Renaissance (1300s–1600s) the Italians thought the aubergine was poisonous and evil. It became known as *mala insana* — 'the unhealthy apple'. In other parts of Europe eating aubergines was suspected to cause madness, leprosy, cancer and bad breath. Louis XIV asked the famous French gardener Jean-Baptiste de La Quintinie (1624–88) to grow them at Versailles and by the eighteenth century the aubergine was an established food in Italy and France. The influential cookery writer Elizabeth David introduced them to the British in the mid-twentieth century.

JULY

*T*he growth spurt that was so obvious in spring and early summer has slowed down and the further north you are, the less time you have to replant and gap up for autumn and winter crops. So every time a gap appears, plug it with a catch crop like lettuce, spinach or dwarf French beans. Although these will take longer to crop now that daylight hours are waning, they should be harvestable by September if you choose the correct variety.

The weather this month will dictate whether you will be weeding or watering and it's important to do both as required. Fortunately the evenings are light. Keep harvesting crops, especially the first beans, to encourage more. Enjoy your glut of home-grown crops, for July is one of the most productive months of all.

1 Cover Up Cauliflower Curds

(*early July*)

CAULIFLOWER is the hardest vegetable of all to grow. It's the most susceptible to club root of all the brassicas, so it should always be raised in modules. It's more attractive to birds, slugs and caterpillars than any other, so it must be netted. It also demands good growing conditions (with lots of nitrogen) and it needs watering and feeding when growing. Finally, it takes up a lot of space. But a home-grown cauliflower is a sweet delicacy and quite different from one that's been commercially grown.

There are three types of variety: summer, autumn and winter. However, most gardeners opt for autumn-cropping varieties that can be harvested in September after the peas and beans have waned. These cauliflowers are sown in April and planted outside in June.

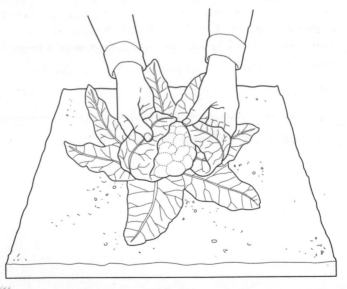

If you're prepared to take the time and trouble, the following technique works. Sow your seeds in modules (one seed in each) and once the plants reach 7.5cm (3in) in height, carefully remove them and put them into small individual pots measuring 7.5–10cm (3–4in) in diameter. Grow these on for a further 2–3 weeks, keeping them well watered.

Prepare the bed well, adding a granular, nitrogen-rich fertilizer just before planting. Tap one or two plants out from their pots and check that the roots have not begun to circle the pot. The roots should be just touching the edges. If they are circling, tease them out. Space each plant 60cm (2ft) apart and net against butter-flies.

Carefully nurture the plants, making sure they have enough water. Then, as the curd develops, fold the large outer leaves over the curd to cover it. This keeps it white – exposure to light can turn it yellow.

Did you know? The cauliflower is thought to have come from Cyprus in the sixteenth century and was considered as exotic as the melon then. Josiah Wedgwood made a cauliflower teapot in 1760, one of the first novelty teapots ever made.

Organic Tip ✔

Variety is everything and the more compact F1 varieties are superior.

2 Fill Gaps with Dwarf French Beans

(early July)

AT THIS time of year gaps start appearing in patches rather than whole rows and the wise vegetable gardener should make use of every inch by sowing catch crops that deliver quickly. Best of all for this purpose are dwarf French beans. Certain varieties can crop in 7 weeks and there's no staking. The nitrogen-fixing roots will also add fertility to your soil, and as soon as the crop is over the beans can be removed easily. Just a few plants produce a heavy crop of beans, enough for several meals, and it's quite possible to lift a single root of potatoes and sow a few beans straight away. Dwarf French beans crop for roughly 4 weeks and probably occupy the ground for 12 weeks or so, so they will be gone by the time autumn preparation starts.

French beans enjoy warm sun and crop more heavily in warmer conditions. I enjoy their flavour and crunchy texture when lightly cooked and added to salads. Pod colour varies between purple, yellow and green, making them look summery on the plate and in the garden, although sadly purple beans cook to dark green.

If you are plugging a gap, sprinkle a few seeds straight down into the soil to a depth of 5cm (2in) and space them out roughly 10cm (4in) apart. Water them well after sowing. If you have enough room for a row, space two rows 38cm (15in) apart and sprinkle seeds lightly along each row, leaving 2.5–5cm (1–2in) between each seed.

Did you know? Although called French beans, these plants originated in South America, where they have been eaten for millennia. They arrived in Europe in the early sixteenth century and, as they became popular in Italy first, they were called Roman beans. However, by the mid-nineteenth century they had become known as French beans, possibly because more breeding was being carried out in France.

SECRETS OF SUCCESS

- Choose a warm, sunny site.
- Slugs adore French beans and the dwarf varieties are so close to the ground that they present little challenge to gastropods. Hoe between plants if possible and always water in the first half of the day — well before slugs become active.
- Pick carefully, because the large leaves hide the beans and if any run to seed it will slow down your crop.
- Green and yellow varieties are speedier to crop than purple-podded ones.
- Water once flowering starts, if it's dry.

VARIETIES

'Stanley'
The fastest-maturing bean I have grown, producing a heavy crop of slender green beans in one flush — which is useful.

'Sonesta' AGM
Compact plants producing a high yield of yellow, waxy beans.

'Purple Tepee'
Purple pods 15cm (6in) in length with a very good flavour. The name is misleading: it does not form a tepee — it's a compact dwarf French bean.

'Delinel' AGM
Slightly mottled green beans on strong plants. Exceptional flavour.

3 Sow Florence Fennel
(mid-July)

FLORENCE fennel provides a real taste of summer with its aniseed flavour. It's also handsome, with swollen cream roots and green feathery foliage. However, it's a tender annual and therefor can be sown only between May and July. It needs warmth and can fail in poor British summers. It also has a tendency to bolt (run to seed) if stressed, but it is worth the gamble. Cold nights encourage bolting and May can be chilly. I prefer to sow it after the longest day when temperatures are more consistent.

Warmth and water are needed in order for the bulbs to swell to a good size and this normally takes 10 weeks from sowing. Gardeners in very warm places can get bulbs that weigh over 500g (1lb). Prepare a drill and sow the seeds directly into the ground, to a depth of 2.5cm (1in), thinning them out after germination to leave 25–30cm (10–12in) between each seedling. Sowing direct is more successful than raising plants in modules.

Once the seeds have germinated, water regularly in dry weather but don't drench your plants because Florence fennel prefers good drainage. Little and often is the key. Fleece in September on cold nights, for this is a warm-season crop, as the name Florence suggests. These are demanding plants to grow, but they crop quickly and the flavour is intensely aromatic when the roots are baked or braised so that the edges caramelize.

> **Did you know?** Florence fennel has been known in England since the eighteenth century when a London nurseryman included it in his seed list. He imported the seeds from Italy, where it is widely grown, but our weather makes growing it rather riskier.

SECRETS OF SUCCESS

- Water regularly – little and often – because this crop enjoys moisture and good drainage.
- Light soil is an advantage.
- Earth the bulbs up (i.e., mound soil up against the developing bulbs) as they develop to keep the skins pale.
- Cut above ground level and then the base will sprout and provide fennel-flavoured foliage which can be used to flavour chicken and fish dishes.

VARIETIES

'Victoria' F1 AGM
Well-filled green-and-white bulbs.

'Zefa Fino' AGM
Fine, feathery foliage and creamy, medium-sized bulbs. Matures quickly.

'Amigo' F1 AGM
Uniform, medium-sized bulbs that swell up early in the season. A paler variety.

'Finale'
Slow to bolt, producing wide, white bulbs with green, feathery leaves.

4 Make Late Sowings of Salads and Roots

(mid-July)

THERE IS still enough time to sow carrots, beetroot and salad crops for late-autumn cropping, especially now that winter usually comes later.

By now most early potatoes are out of the ground, or partly out. If sowing or planting after potatoes, rake the area thoroughly and water the ground well if it's dry. Then apply blood, fish and bone (see page 158) to boost the nutrients. Potatoes leave the soil exhausted and their foliage often prevents rain from penetrating the ground.

Lettuces sown straight into the ground should germinate within 10 days unless we have a heatwave. Hot temperatures do delay the germination of lettuce seeds, so be prepared to repeat-sow if necessary. You can also sow seeds in 6 × 4 modular trays, one or two in each module, and then plant those out once their roots have reached the bottom. Good varieties for this time of year include Cos lettuces – the narrow, slender ones with an upright habit. These are less likely to bolt and turn bitter than other types and some varieties show excellent mildew tolerance. These lettuces can be eaten from September until November if they are watered during August, so they are well worth the effort.

Beetroot and carrots also grow well in warm, damp conditions and the second half of summer often provides the perfect climate. However, if August is dry you will have to water both. Sown now, they will produce young roots in late October. Certain winter-hardy carrots can be left in the ground and then dug as needed.

Did you know? The earliest lettuces were almost certainly weeds, because gardeners allowed weeds to develop between their crops and then harvested the weeds whilst they waited for the crops. The Cos (or Roman) lettuce is depicted on Egyptian tomb plaques dating back to 3000 BC and it was eaten and used as a medicinal cure-all.

Organic Tip ✔

When harvesting leafy crops like lettuce and cabbage, always lift the whole plant before cutting. A stump left in the ground can harbour diseases.

SECRETS OF SUCCESS

- Vigorous F1 varieties of carrot and beetroot are best for summer sowing because their growth and germination rate are much faster than others'.
- Be extra rigorous about thinning these crops as they need to mature quickly. They do not have time to fight it out.
- Water well.
- Harvest the first roots when still small by taking from all along the row — this will leave more space for the others.
- Earth up the roots as you harvest — this helps in dry weather.

5 Sow Spring Cabbages
(late July)

IT'S TIME to sow spring cabbages for harvesting from next March onwards. These can either provide open heads of rich green leaves (as in spring greens) or in the case of some varieties be left to head up to form small conical heads. Spring cabbages fill the gap between Brussels sprouts and purple sprouting broccoli, although this does depend on weather. They provide tasty leaves with a sweet flavour and can be harvested until June, before other crops are ready.

Seeds can be sown in modules or in a seedbed in the ground. However, seeds won't germinate in high temperatures, so if you are using the greenhouse try to find a cool position.

Seedlings should be planted out once they have five or six leaves – usually when 10cm (4in) high. Early September is the optimum moment, although those with warm gardens can get away with planting in the first half of October. Compact varieties can be planted 30cm (12in) apart; larger varieties are best spaced 45cm (18in) apart.

Brassicas prefer firm soil and spring cabbages should not be fed. They need to develop slowly. For this reason you shouldn't apply a nitrogen-rich fertilizer, which would promote immediate leafy growth that would be vulnerable in frosts. Net against birds and caterpillars.

Did you know? The Ancient Greeks and Romans grew and ate cabbages, and the statesman Cato the Elder (234–149 BC) advocated their medicinal use for cleansing and strengthening the body long before their antioxidant properties were discovered by modern scientists.

Organic Tip ✔

Spring cabbage does most of its growing over winter when pests and diseases are not around. The right timing, though, is imperative. The plants need to be large enough to get through winter but small enough not to begin hearting up until spring.

SECRETS OF SUCCESS

- Find a warm, sunny position so that your cabbage plants have the best chance of growing and surviving in hard weather.
- Net to prevent bird and butterfly damage.
- Firm the soil down well after planting and after windy weather. Earthing up the stem helps to prevent wind rock.
- Do not feed your spring cabbage plants.

6 Sow Spinach, Perpetual Spinach and Chard

(late July)

THESE THREE vegetables could provide you with leafy vegetables from late September right through the winter if sown now. Spinach is an annual that is in the ground for 3 months or so. Certain F1 varieties are vigorous enough to germinate quickly and give you perfect spinach throughout autumn; the leaves are lush and never bitter. The best two varieties for sowing now are 'Scenic' and 'Toscane', both of which can be sown right up until late August. Most varieties are only moderately hardy, but 'Triathlon' will often overwinter to provide spring leaves.

Perpetual spinach is a hardy biennial that will stay in the ground for up to 2 years. The leaves are edible and taste like spinach, although the tough mid-ribs and stems should be removed. Swiss chard is closely related, but it has thick, celery-like stems that come in white, yellow, orange or red. The stems have a salty, beetroot flavour and they are cooked separately from the leaves. The crinkled, shiny foliage tastes like spinach.

Swiss chard is extremely hardy and makes an excellent crop for spring and late autumn; you can cut and come again, often when little else is available. The plants need plenty of space and it's usual to leave a 30cm (12in) between each. This crop can look very handsome and colourful. Rhubarb chard has bright-red stems, while Rainbow chard comes in a mixture of colours.

Did you know? Spinach is mentioned in the first known English cookbook, *The Forme of Cury* (1390), where it is referred to as 'spinnedge' and 'spynoches'. In 1533, when Catherine de Medici (1518–89) became Queen of France, she insisted that spinach should be served at every meal. Many French dishes that include spinach are known as 'Florentine', reflecting Catherine's birthplace in Florence.

SECRETS OF SUCCESS

- Sow crops in warm, sunny positions to encourage good germination.
- Sow thinly and then always thin. Leave 7.5cm (3in) gaps between leaf spinach, 22cm (9in) between perpetual spinach, and 30cm (12in) between chard plants.
- All these crops enjoy moisture, so water them well in dry weather.
- Choose F1 spinach varieties with mildew resistance.
- Fertility is also important, so add a general fertilizer when planting.
- Six Swiss chard plants are normally enough. The white-stemmed varieties are hardier than the more colourful ones.

VARIETIES

**Spinach
'Toscane' F1 AGM**
Rounded, thickly textured, dark-green leaves. This is the most successful spinach for repeat sowings from April until September. Mildew-resistant.

**Spinach
'Triathlon' F1 AGM**
Large, pointed, yellow-green leaves. A strong variety for cooking.

**Spinach
'Scenic' F1 AGM**
Bright-green leaves that can be cooked or eaten as baby leaves. Mildew-resistant.

**Swiss Chard
'Lucullus' AGM**
Light-green, crinkled foliage and ivory-white stems.

Organic Tip ✔

Pick regularly, as this sends a message to your plant to produce more new leaves rather than flowers.

AUGUST

Now that the days are shorter the evening dews, produced by cooler temperatures, are reviving tired crops. However, they may look fresher than they really are, so if it's dry keep up the watering. Soak rather than sprinkle. Carry on picking too. Give it away if it's all too much. If a holiday heckons, ask a neighbour or friend to pick your beans: this will keep your beans in flower.

The weeds will have slowed down, but as soon as there's a note of autumn in the air there will be a rush of seedlings, so don't stop hoeing and weeding. If it has been a good year, you should be in a land of plenty by August and by the end of the month your plot will have taken on a gentle, almost decadent air.

1 Lift Garlic, Onions and Shallots

(early August)

THE BULBOUS members of the Allium family should all be ready or almost ready to lift. As soon as you see the foliage begin to yellow and flag, it's time to act. If you leave these even 10 days too long they may re-sprout in heavy rain. That makes the bulbs impossible to store, as a green shoot forms in the heart of the bulb.

Shallots should now be fully grown and splaying their bulbs out in a cluster. Onions should also be a good size by now. In sunny summers the ripening process turns the leaves yellow; in wet summers the drying process may need a little encouragement. Lift the bulbs away from the soil with a fork so that the shallow roots break contact with the soil. Leave them in the ground like this for 2 weeks or so and then gather them up. Space them out on a slatted bench or table in full sun. Once the skins are dry and papery, store them in a garden shed.

Garlic should be harvested as soon as the leaves go floppy, which can happen from the end of June until now, depending on when it was planted. The bulbs usually lie underground, so lift them carefully because garlic bruises easily. Shake off the soil and place them somewhere warm and dry before storing.

Organic Tip ✔

The size of your onions is determined by the spaces between them. For a medium-sized onion, space the sets at 10cm (4in). Do not bend the stems over — it encourages neck rot.

Did you know? The Egyptians grew and ate garlic and records from 3200 BC tell us that they regarded it as a sacred plant. Clay models of garlic bulbs were placed in the tomb of Tutankhamun, whether to ward off evil (as it is with vampires) or for its aphrodisiac qualities we shall probably never know. However, aristocratic Greeks and Romans refused to eat garlic, although they fed it to their soldiers and workmen to make them more aggressive.

ONIONS AND GARLICS

Elephant Garlic
This is not true garlic – it is closely related to the leek instead. However, it forms huge bulbs containing four or five large, mild-flavoured cloves which can be roasted. Plant in autumn. Store until Christmas.

Garlic 'Iberian Wight'
Large, flat white garlic with purple stripes from south-west Spain. Plant much deeper than most – to 6cm (2½in) depth – as this variety pushes upwards. Store until January.

Garlic 'Albigensian Wight'
Large, white, flat-topped garlic from south-west France, eaten by the Cathars in the thirteenth century. Keeps until February – a month longer than other varieties.

Onion 'Sturon' AGM
The best round, golden onion for storage.

For more garlic varieties, see February, page 22.

2 Potato Care
(early August)

AUGUST is the month when potato blight takes hold, encouraged
by warm, humid summer weather – technically known as 'Smith
periods' (see overleaf). The spores are carried on the air, so the
disease sweeps over whole areas very quickly. It constantly mutates
and potato varieties that once showed resistance may well succumb
in the future. It is a headache for breeders and growers.

The first sign is slightly floppy foliage, followed by yellow
marks and brown spotting. As soon as you see it, cut the tops off
and bin or destroy them to prevent further spread. Do not add
them to the compost heap. Cutting off the foliage quickly will limit
the disease and, hopefully, protect the tubers. Infected tubers turn
brown and rot. Try not to confuse this with natural yellowing when
dying back – look for the brown lesions.

Potatoes are members of the Solanum family and the disease
can spread to other members of the family, including outdoor
tomatoes and aubergines. For this reason try not to place these two
crops close to potatoes.

Wild potato species tend to be blight-resistant, and 'Sarpo' potatoes, bred by the Savari family, are now becoming available. Other varieties show great resistance. Not all get blighted tubers, so hunting out blight-resistant varieties is a good idea. Also, many gardeners who grow only first early and second early varieties avoid the disease altogether because by the time it strikes the potatoes are all out of the ground.

Did you know? A 'Smith period' is a 48-hour period in which the minimum temperature is 10°C (50°F) or more and the relative humidity exceeds 90 per cent for at least 11 hours on each day.

Organic Tip ✔

It is almost impossible to buy an organic potato due to potato blight. On average, a commercial potato crop is sprayed against blight approximately sixteen times, so growing your own is well worth it.

BLIGHT-RESISTANT VARIETIES

'Valor' (maincrop)
Oval, creamy-fleshed potato, for all culinary uses. Very disease-resistant. Also good in dry soil.

'Cara' (maincrop)
The ultimate allotment potato, with very rounded, pink-eyed tubers. A high-yielding, floury potato for every use. The firm tubers store really well, rarely succuming to blight.

'Lady Balfour' (second early)
Pink-splashed, oval tubers with a firm texture. Heavy-yielding potato for roasting and boiling.

'Sante' (maincrop)
Oval, creamy-fleshed potato for boiling and baking. Resists blight in tubers.

- Stick to early or blight-resistant varieties.
- Rotate your crops on a 4-year cycle (see page 156) to lessen the chance of disease.
- Remove all the potatoes from the ground when you harvest and dig up any sleepers that pop up next year — they could be harbouring the disease.
- Don't water the foliage after the middle of July. Water the ground with a leaky hose instead so that the foliage stays dry.
- If you get blight, cut off the tops immediately.

3 Stop Tomatoes
(mid-August)

IN THEIR native land tomatoes are short-lived perennials, but we grow them in the summer months only because they are frost-tender. Consequently, they will carry on flowering, but you'll get much better fruit if you restrict the number of trusses by pinching out the tops or side shoots now.

Six trusses is usually a good number for varieties grown under glass. However, outdoor tomatoes are generally restricted to only three or four trusses. Once 'stopped' the plant puts all its energy into plumping up the fruits and the quality of each tomato improves. You don't want a triffid that flowers into late November: the fruit will be tasteless and your plants will get disease. Go for quality not quantity – a good maxim for all vegetable-growing.

Keep up the fortnightly feeding of liquid potash-rich food (either branded tomato food or free comfrey tea – see page 69) until the end of the month, then begin to restrict the watering slightly. Remove any large leaves that are shielding fruit trusses; that way all the fruit should ripen.

I like all my greenhouse tomatoes to be out of the ground by late October. This gives enough time to enrich the area with compost ready for planting out winter salad in their place. Outdoor tomatoes will also be picked in September and, although they are a gamble, they are still worth growing. The flavour is always more intense. Early-cropping F1 outdoor varieties are more desirable.

Did you know? This red fruit was regarded with great suspicion until the mid–eighteenth century. However, the American president Thomas Jefferson (1743–1826) grew 'tomatoes', as he called them, in his Monticello garden in 1780 and that is where they first became popular to eat. Heritage American varieties include 'Brandywine' and 'Paragon' – but they tend to be difficult to grow in the cooler parts of Britain.

SECRETS OF SUCCESS

- Get the watering regime right (indoors and out) and try to establish a routine. If tomatoes get too dry and then suffer a deluge, the fruit splits. This attracts disease.
- Feed religiously with liquid tomato food or comfrey tea (see page 69) once the first fruit appears. Every 2 weeks works well.
- Try to use cans of sun-warmed water in early summer to emulate the steamy riversides of South America where tomatoes grow naturally.
- Put tomatoes outside in June (at the earliest) and give them a warm, sheltered position where afternoon sun strikes. Midday sun can cause stress.
- Select early-cropping varieties for outdoors so that they produce fruit before mid-August when potato blight begins to devastate tomatoes and aubergines.
- Seek out blight-tolerant varieties. Many of these are being introduced from eastern Europe.
- Fleece on cool September nights so that the plants do not get checked by cold weather.

BLIGHT-RESISTANT VARIETIES

'Red Alert'
A bush variety that is early, prolific and tasty – but slugs can be a problem due to its low growth habit.

'Alicante'
This cordon variety normally recommended for growing under glass will also crop outdoors, producing shiny-skinned, medium-sized fruit with a good flavour.

For greenhouse varieties, see May (page 66); for outdoor varieties, see June (page 43).

4 Use Compost to Mulch after Rain

(*mid-August*)

HOPEFULLY your compost heap has been working well all summer long. You should be able to feel the warmth through your fingertips, and the level should certainly have fallen. Try to dig it out now, because the next month or two will provide a glut of green material as crops are harvested and cleared.

Well-rotted compost should look crumbly and dark, and smell sweet. If you have material like this at this time of the year, apply it to the soil surface now, making sure that the ground is damp. It will feed your crops and act as a mulch, keeping moisture in. At this time of year a layer of compost soon disappears into the ground, pulled down by worms. It is important to make sure that the plants you mulch are fully grown, as slugs will home in on any tender babies.

The advantage of emptying your compost bin now is that you create space at a time of year when leafy waste is in plentiful supply and the temperatures are still warm. You can get more compost quickly if you can add matierals that contain a good balance of nutrients. Having three compost bins is ideal. One full one can be covered up and left to rot down. One can be ongoing, with material being added every few days. Use the empty bin to turn the full one into, by forking it over into the space. Turning aerates the mixture and brings the well-rotted middle out, allowing the outer edges a better chance to rot down.

Did you know? Composting is an ancient art. The people of Mesopotamia were doing it 1,000 years before Moses was born. There are references to composting in the Talmud, in the Old Testament and in ancient Chinese writings. The Ancient Greeks practised composting, taking straw from animal stalls and burying it in cultivated fields.

Organic Tip ✔

Mulching keeps in the moisture but the ground must be damp. However, as the top layer decomposes it uses up nitrogen from the ground below. So if you are using a material like bark (which rots down very slowly), dust the ground with a nitrogen-rich fertilizer like powdered chicken manure (sold as 6X) before mulching.

SECRETS OF SUCCESS

- Site your compost bin somewhere warm.
- Keep the compost moist and covered – opened-up cardboard boxes are ideal.
- Chop large pieces of green material with a spade or invest in a shredder.
- Feel the heap regularly. The time to turn it is when the heap begins to cool down. Turning is the key to quicker compost.
- Do not add too many grass clippings and always try to rot them partially down first before adding them (see page 85).

- Refrain from adding pernicious weeds such as bindweed and the invasive grass commonly called couch grass or squitch (*Elymus repens*).
- Do not add weeds or flowers that seed heavily (like foxgloves, poppies and aquilegias) to garden compost.
- Aim for a layered sandwich (with airy gaps) and add natural accelerators.
- Do not add cooked food unless you wish to attract rats.
- Dog and cat faeces are too acidic and a health risk.
- Do not add diseased green material to your heap. If it looks blighted or virused, get rid of it. Mildewed material could be added.

GOOD COMPOST BINS

The square wooden bins (1.2 x 1.2 x 1.2 metres/4 x 4 x 4ft) with lift-off fronts are the Rolls Royces of compost bins. Smaller heaps do not warm up effectively.

Plastic bins are easier for people with smaller gardens, where space is at a premium.

Compost tumblers are useful if turning the heap is difficult for you. They can make compost within 6 weeks.

Worm composters can be kept under-cover, and the vermi-compost is very rich in nutrients, but the expense of setting one up puts off most large garden owners.

5 Sow Japanese Onions
(late August)

IF YOU want onions by midsummer next year you should sow the seeds of Japanese onions now. These hardy onions (mainly bred in Japan and also known as overwintering onions) will come through bad winters, although they often look very shabby. They need only 12 hours of daylight to trigger bulbing up, so they grow actively from the March equinox until ready for harvest in June.

Conventional onion varieties need 16 hours of daylight before nature tells them to start storing food.

Only keen vegetable gardeners bother to grow Japanese onions because they do not store: they need to be used as you dig them, so one row is enough for most families. At first these are varieties were available only in seed form. Seeds sown *in situ* in shallow drills 23cm (9in) apart. and the seedlings are thinned out to 10cm (4in) apart in the following spring. You can also sow seeds in modules under glass. Place roughly seven seeds in each and plant out the entire module in the second half of September. However, sets are now available too. These are planted in early October.

Did you know? Thinly sliced onions soaked in a bowl of cold water for 30 minutes taste sweeter and the slices keep for longer.

SECRETS OF SUCCESS

- Timing is everything. Sow Japanese onions in the last third of August. Any earlier and they will bolt in May.
- September is too late to sow: they will not be large enough or well-rooted enough to overwinter.
- Water well after sowing or planting. Water again in March in dry springs as the bulbs need to swell.
- Keep them well weeded.
- The weather will dictate the success of this crop.

Organic Tip ✔

If you suffer from onion diseases like mildew, do not attempt to grow overwintering onions, as you will keep the disease going in your garden throughout the year.

6 Sow Green Manure
(late August)

GREEN MANURE crops are an effective way of enriching the soil. The most successful are the short-term green manures that germinate quickly and are then dug in over winter. They can be sown now and dug into the ground in 2–3 months in a leafy state. Some long-term varieties (such as alfalfa), which stay in the ground for 2–3 years, have long tap roots that penetrate the ground. Although the deep roots bring nutrients up to the topsoil, these can be extremely hard to get rid of. In any case, most gardeners cannot afford to tie up the ground for this long.

Green manures can be very useful to the gardener because they smother the surface and exclude weeds. On light soil they prevent soil erosion, stop nutrients leaching out of the soil and enrich the soil. If you can dig them in young, they will decompose quickly. However, if they get too tall and the work looks onerous, you can mow the top growth off, allow it to re-sprout a little and then dig it in. This decision will depend on whether you want to use the ground next spring. Bulky material is likely to take a full

year to decompose. In August green manures germinate quickly, but as September wears on germination can slow down. If you plant late you risk unwanted seeds popping up in spring. Choosing which green manure to use is vital. Some are more suitable for spring sowing than autumn sowing. Weeds are also a green manure in themselves – but all too often they set seed quickly, so they must be dug in before they flower.

Did you know? Lupins were the original green manure. The Incas used them over 2,000 years ago to protect and enrich the soil and to prevent soil erosion.

Organic Tip ✔

Green manures increase the percentage of organic matter in the soil and improve water retention and soil structure.

SECRETS OF SUCCESS

- Choose your crop carefully. It is the quick crops that are sown now. Long-term green manures tend to be spring-sown.
- Many green manures are nitrogen-fixing legumes. Extra nitrogen can be added by sprinkling blood, fish and bone (see page 158) or by using pelleted chicken manure. Don't discount easier green manures like phacelia. It's the extra organic matter that they add that is most desirable.
- Sow in damp weather for better germination.
- Dig the crop in before it flowers.

GREEN MANURES

Mustard (*Sinapsis alba*)
This is the fastest green manure crop, but it runs to seed quickly. It's frost-prone, so it almost dies off, leaving little work. It is the simplest green manure — although it is a brassica, so don't grow it if you have club root.

Purple Tansy (*Phacelia tanacetifolia*)
This germinates easily in warm soil and produces growth quickly. Once there's a covering, dig it in because in mild winters it will flower and set seed.

Red Clover (*Trifolium incarnatum*)
Sow in autumn for digging in during spring; or sow in spring for digging in during autumn. It sweetens and also helps to lighten heavy soils, and it provides a great deal of organic matter. You need to dig this in thoroughly.

Fenugreek (*Trigonella foenum-graecum*)
This half-hardy annual grows very quickly and produces lots of leaves. When dug in, these enrich the soil.

AUTUMN TASKS

To Do

Explore the depths of the
compost heap and empty as
much as you can

Cut and ripen squashes and
pumpkins

Cut down asparagus as it yellows

Lift all potatoes by the end of
September

Weed and clear old crops

Begin winter digging

Collect leaves

Check nets on brassicas –
hungry pigeons are about

Sow under Glass

Oriental salad leaves, radicchio
and endive for winter use

Spinach

Sow Outside

'Aquadulce Claudia' broad beans
(early November)

'Feltham First' peas (early
November)

Plant

Elephant garlic and autumn-
sown varieties of garlic

Transplant spring cabbages

SEPTEMBER

Ask a gardener which is their favourite month and many will automatically reply September. Whether it's the quality of the light, which has a special magic in early autumn; or the satisfaction that the worst of the work is over; or perhaps it's the glut of produce September always brings. Whatever the reason, it's a contented, mellow month if you're a gardener.

September frequently brings the first frost, however, then there is often a long gap before the second one comes along. If you can cover outdoor, frost-tender plants like courgettes, cucumbers, peppers and tomatoes with newspaper or fleece during cold nights, you can often keep them going for several more weeks.

1 Sow Winter Salads
(early September)

YEARS AGO salads were purely summer affairs, but in recent years cold-tolerant leaves have become a garden staple. Plant them in an unheated greenhouse or frame and they will produce a crop from October right through to next April, and they are very happy to follow on after tomatoes. Oriental vegetables (like mizuna and pak choi) thrive in cool temperatures and you can plant them alongside rocket, endive, chicory and winter lettuces. Seeds are sown now and young plants should go out in the second half of September or in October (after lifting tomatoes). By then the temperatures are much lower, so there are few slugs and other pests about. The low temperatures also ensure slow growth. Crops that are prone to bolt (run to seed) in summer, such as rocket, will grow on for months, producing leaf after leaf without flowering. And there's no flea beetle either!

Seed companies sell mixtures that vary in flavour from hot and spicy to mild, but you can also create your own mixtures. The easiest technique is to use modules for each variety and place two or three seeds in each. This will save pricking out. Bed out the plant clusters in rows, leaving 10cm (4in) between them. This creates a carpet of leaves, and the textures and colours will vary pleasingly from rounded, deep-green baby spinach to ferny red mizuna and peppery rocket.

Organic Tip ✔

Place upturned plant saucers among your leaves. Slugs will hide under them, making it easy for you to find them. They are especially partial to chicory leaves.

> **Did you know?** Bagged supermarket salads have been found to contain potentially harmful bacteria like *E. coli*.

SECRETS OF SUCCESS

- Sprinkle on blood, fish and bone (see page 158) once the plot is clear. This will boost the soil's nitrogen content.
- Once the plants are in the ground, water them thoroughly every other morning so that they race away.
- Once the plants reach a height of 10cm (4in), pick them regularly to encourage more leaves.
- If you spot any plants running to seed, pick out the tops.

VARIETIES

'Niche Oriental Mixed'
Golden and red mustards, mizuna, komatsuna and rocket. Mizuna is almost fern-like in leaf and komatsuna resembles small-leaved spinach. Both add great flavour and texture as well as looking pretty on the plate.

Rocket
'Apollo'
Peppery tender leaves of just the right size.

Chicory
'Radicchio di Treviso'
Upright dark-red leaves with white mid-ribs – a bitter flavour.

Chicory
'Grumolo Verde'
Rosette-forming, green-leaved chicory that tends to come into its own as the days lengthen.

2 Repair Grass Paths, etc.
(early September)

GRASS PATHS are more environmentally friendly and kinder to ground-hugging friendly predators such as ground and rove beetles. This is the best time to tackle grass repairs – whether it's seeding the gaps in paths or dealing with the weeds. The temperatures are ideal now – not too hot and not too cold. Nighttime dew encourages germination and autumn rains boost growth because the soil is still warm. Spring, the other opportunity to sow grass seed, is chancier as the nighttime temperatures can be low and spring droughts often occur.

The first thing to do is to remove all perennial weeds, especially dandelion roots; there are specialist tools for this job called daisy grubbers. Distress the bare patches with a short-tined rake or fork, treading it down very lightly before scattering the seeds. Water well, cover with wire netting and keep off the area for 6 weeks. The ground should be kept watered throughout this time, but shouldn't get waterlogged.

Larger areas will need better preparation. Rotavate the area if possible, or dig it through by hand, removing any stones and all weeds. Either add organic material to poor soil, or add grit or sand to heavy clay. Leave the ground to settle for 10 days, then hoe off any emerging weeds. Sow the seeds as instructed on the packet.

Lawn seed mostly contains two main types of grass. Rye grass is tough and fast growing, and therefore quick to establish. Fescues are finer and slower growing, and best for ornamental 'bowling green' lawns. The best option for paths is a mixture containing both.

VARIETIES IN LAWN MIXTURES

Perennial Rye Grass (*Lolium perrine*)

Rye grass is tough and durable and is found in many mixtures. It germinates within 10 days and forms a dense lawn. It dislikes shade and isn't drought-tolerant, but quickly bounces back after rain.

Fescue (*Festuca species*)

Several different fescues can be included in mixtures. These fine-leaved grasses thrive in well-drained soil in the wild. They form the basis of fine lawn mixtures, but they are also contained in family lawn mixtures to a lesser degree. They are slower growing and tend to stay green in dry weather.

Browntop Bent (*Agrostis species*)

This fine green grass is added to mixtures designed to thrive in shady areas.

Smooth-Stalked Meadow Grass (*Poa pratensis*)

Another grass for shade, with drought tolerance. This grey-green grass may take 21 days to come up.

Did you know? The lawnmower was invented in 1830 by Edwin Beard Budding, an engineer from Stroud in Gloucestershire. He saw a machine trimming cloth in a local weaving mill and realized that it could cut grass in the same way.

- Choose the right mixture. One recommended for everyday family use makes an ideal path between vegetable plots. Make sure it's fresh.
- Catch the weather and sow after rain if possible, otherwise water first.
- Don't be mean with the seeds, and rake through after sowing so that the seeds are in close contact with the soil.
- Cover with wire and then fleece to keep the warmth in. Leave the fleece down for a week.
- If germination fails after 20 days, sow again quickly.

3 Harvest Sweetcorn
(mid-September)

ONE CROP that breeders have revolutionized in recent years is sweetcorn. Modern F1 varieties now crop reliably in Britain even in colder areas if planted out in June and watered well. Many of the best British-bred varieties are named after birds. They include 'Lark', a mid-season variety; 'Kite', a later variety; and 'Lapwing', which comes between the two. These extra-tender varieties are almost fibreless: they will not fill your teeth with annoying bits and the bright-yellow cobs cook quickly. Of the three, 'Lark' is particularly recommended for colder gardens and every cob seems to be well filled.

Cobs of corn are very sweet. However, after picking the sugars turn to starch quickly, so always eat your cobs straight away. Supersweet varieties are not necessarily sweeter, but they take longer to lose their sugars. Consequently they are favoured by some commercial growers because the cobs can be stored for longer. Home gardeners should stick to the extra-tender varieties and 'Lark' F1 is the best at the moment. Once the beards are brown the cobs are ripe, but if in doubt pinch a kernel and it will yield a milky fluid if ripe.

Most varieties yield one or two cobs per plant and these should be harvested when ripe. Lift sweetcorn plants and compost as soon as possible.

Did you know? In Latin America sweetcorn is tradition-ally eaten with beans. Each plant is deficient in an essential amino acid, but it is abundant in the other. Together they form a balanced diet.

Organic Tip ✔

Sweetcorn foliage and stems are cellulose-rich and take a long time to rot down. Snip them into pieces as you add them to the compost heap — this helps them to decompose more quickly.

SECRETS OF SUCCESS

- Sweetcorn is wind-pollinated, so grow only one variety to prevent cross-fertilization.
- Plant in a block (not a line) to aid pollination.
- The secret of a good crop is watering in June and July to create lots of foliage and height.
- If you have a glut, don't store cobs. Cook and freeze the surplus instead.

4 The Autumn Tidy
(mid-September)

COOLER nights followed by warm days are a recipe for dewy mornings and evenings. These conditions are perfect for the re-emergence of the slug and snail. These are not all bad. The larger slugs do eat debris, but it makes sense to begin to tidy up the vegetable garden so that there are no hiding places. By mid-September the garden has begun to move towards decay and decline, and many crops are coming to an end.

Frosts are not far away and the slightest one will reduce cucurbits to mush, so if you have any courgettes that look well past their best, or any cucumbers at the end of their productive life, it's better to compost them now before they become slimy to handle. Nasturtiums and rhubarb leaves also go to mush, so tidy the crowns of rhubarb and bin any nasturtiums. Tidy up the brassica bed and remove any fallen yellowing leaves.

Weeds will also be germinating apace and hoeing this month will disrupt them, as well as disturbing any slug and snail eggs in your soil. Do a thorough job now and it will save you hours next spring because weeds develop seeds within a short space of time.

SECRETS OF SUCCESS

- The gullies around vegetable beds (where the lawn or path meets the soil) are seed repositories for weeds and shelter belts for slugs. Clean them out now. Trim the grass and re-cut the edges. It will prevent a lot of problems.
- Tidy rhubarb crowns and compost cucurbits before frost makes them flop and flag.
- Hoe your vegetable beds to keep down the weeds. You will also disturb slug eggs – the birds love them.
- Collect leaves and put them into a wire frame or punctured black plastic sacks. They will slowly form leaf compost, which makes a good mulch.

USEFUL TOOLS

Rubber Rake
Much better and friendlier than a noisy leaf vacuum, this wide rake has rubber tines that can be dragged through plants without damaging them. It's a wizard at collecting leaves from the soil.

Small Onion Hoe
A vital tool for getting between onions or brassicas. The one-sided blade is less dangerous than the swoe.

Swoe
A stainless-steel blade with a double edge that cuts as you go backwards and forwards. This is an excellent tool for weeding bare plots, where you can push it up and down without fear of decapitating plants. Leave the weeds on the soil surface if they aren't flowering and then dig them in as a green manure.

Wheelbarrow
Choose something light, durable and not too garish, with a strong pneumatic tyre and good handles. As with gloves and hats, you have to try them out.

Did you know? Snails hibernate in sealed shells and cluster together in sheltered places from October to March. However, slugs are active whenever the temperature is above 5°C (41°F).

5 To Dig or Not to Dig?
(late September)

THERE ARE gardeners who dig and gardeners who don't, and there are good reasons for both. No-dig gardeners believe that nutrients should be added to the surface (in the form of a top-dressing) and pulled down by worms. This definitely leads to warmer soil early in the year, because you are not exposing it to the cold, and fewer weed seeds germinate in spring. No-dig gardeners feel their approach keeps nutrients in the ground. The no-dig method is not labour-free, however, and you have to be prepared to barrow in organic matter to cover the plots with a 5cm (2in) layer once or twice a year.

Most gardeners enjoy digging and believe it aerates the soil and improves soil structure. If you are a digger by nature, this is the best time to start – just as the first frosts arrive. The technique is to get a good fork and turn the soil over once. The clods of soil should not be broken down into a fine tilth – they should be left on the surface in large lumps. This increases the surface area of the soil exposed to the weather. The action of freezing and thawing (brought about by frosts) breaks the clumps down for you over winter. All that the gardener needs to do is rake the soil into a tilth in spring.

Did you know? Ruth Stout (1884–1980), who gardened in Kansas, was a famous no-dig pioneer. She advocated using a thick, 20cm (8in) mulch of hay to suppress weeds and keep the soil moist. Stout used cheap 'spoiled' hay that wasn't suitable for animal use. When she planted potatoes she chitted them and threw them on to the surface, and she planted seeds in the same easy way. She also became famous for not watering her garden for 35 years — and Kansas is a dry place in summer.

SECRETS OF SUCCESS
FOR A NO-DIG APPROACH

- Have a well-prepared source of organic matter — compost or well-rotted manure will do.
- Apply it thinly, aiming to cover to a depth of 5cm (2in).
- Remove perennial weeds (like docks) with a trowel.
- Kill couch grass, dandelions and buttercups by covering them with cardboard.
- Hoe annual weeds in spring when they germinate.
- Root crops like potatoes and parsnips are dug out of the ground, so there is always some soil disturbance even in a no-dig system.
- Raise your vegetable plants in modules in the greenhouse, then plant them out into the garden at the optimum moment so that they get the best start.

6 Lift All Potatoes
(late September)

ALL YOUR potatoes should be lifted before the end of this month so
that they don't attract slugs, which will pepper any tubers left in the
ground with unattractive holes. The potato plant, sensing the
underground attack, fights back by making the potatoes less palat-
able. Affected tubers develop an unpleasant, earthy aroma which
you can taste and smell. This can make them almost inedible.

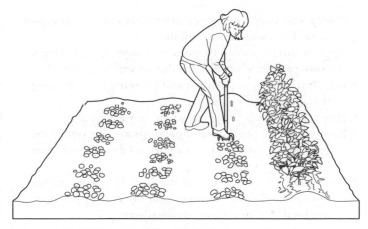

Cut the potato foliage off and allow the ground to dry. Try to
find a dry morning to lift the tubers and leave them for a few hours

to dry off in the air. Store them in thick paper sacks to keep out the light. If sunlight gets to the tubers, they produce chlorophyll and turn green. As they do so, they produce a bitter neurotoxin called solanine as another defence mechanism. Green potatoes look unpalatable and they can upset the stomach. Some potatoes also produce tomato-like fruits and these are toxic, so be sure to dispose of any lying on the ground.

Store only firm, healthy-looking tubers. If any have marks or dark patches on their skin they may be suffering from potato blight. Discard them. If you've grown different varieties, separate them out into different labelled bags because this makes cooking easier. If you have several varieties they will cook at different rates, whether boiled or baked.

Storage times vary according to type. First early and second early varieties generally do not store well, so use these as quickly as you can. Maincrops should store until after Christmas and possibly into March. However, the tubers are frost-prone, so you will need to find a cold but frost-free place to store them, ideally with temperatures around 5°C (41°F).

SECRETS OF SUCCESS

- Thick paper sacks are best. They should be only half-filled. This makes it easier to tip them out and check for bad potatoes. Often the smell alone will tell you.
- Store different varieties in different bags for ease of use.
- Check all stored crops regularly.
- Aim to use up home-grown potatoes by March, as they will begin sprouting as the days lengthen. Commercial crops are sprayed with an anti-sprouting chemical.

Did you know? Each cubic metre of soil contains on average up to 200 slugs, but the amount of rainfall and your type of soil affects how many you may have. They breed all year round, but egg-laying peaks in March–April and September–October.

Organic Tip ✔

Choose your varieties wisely: some are much less attractive to slugs and many of these types are also resistant to eel-worm. If you find slugs have been wreaking havoc with your crop, treat the ground with slug nematodes quickly whilst the soil is still warm enough (see page 58). This will prevent the underground army moving on to other crops.

SLUG-RESISTANT VARIETIES

'Anya'
A knobbly salad potato that can be treated as a second early or left in the ground.

'Cara'
This allotment maincrop toughie seems to hold little attraction for the slug.

'King Edward'
An early maincrop with high slug resistance.

'Sante'
An early maincrop widely grown organically in Europe due to its slug and disease resistance.

'Pentland Dell'
Slug-resistant heavy cropper producing white potatoes.

'Kestrel'
A handsome blue-eyed potato often seen on the show bench. Also slug resistant.

OCTOBER

O ctober is usually a month of warm days and much cooler nights. Winter could descend at any moment, and yet the warmer weather of recent years has meant that crops can continue to grow until November. It's worth protecting any slightly tender or young vegetables with thick horticultural fleece, a light blanket or a double-thickness of newspaper should a frost be forecast. Remove the covering the following morning (if possible) to allow any cold air to escape. If the weather stays mild, then winter squashes, later sowings of beans and courgettes might carry on for a few more valuable weeks.

As crops finish, be tidy and remove them. Take the garden paraphernalia away too – the wigwams of canes that supported beans, for instance. This will make the vegetable garden look better, save time later and preserve your materials. It will also lessen the chance of fungal diseases and the real enemy – slugs – will have nowhere to hide.

1 Cut Back and Weed Asparagus

(early October)

ASPARAGUS is a perennial crop that can stay in the same position for 20 years, so do look after it. Cut the ferny stems down once the foliage begins to yellow; this usually occurs after the first savage frost. Don't add the foliage to the compost heap: it may be harbouring asparagus beetle. Leave 2.5cm (1in) of growth showing, then weed the bed carefully by hand because asparagus is shallow-rooted. Add a thin layer of organic mulch, making sure you put it over warm soil. This will rot down and feed the crowns.

Mulching will also discourage seedlings from germinating next spring. Self-seeding asparagus plants can be a nuisance. If you spot any small seedlings, remove them all, as they will form inferior plants.

You can grow asparagus from seed, but this takes a year longer, so most gardeners choose to plant crowns. You will need at least thirty crowns to get a reasonable crop in the 6-week cutting season and these take up a sizeable area: crowns should be given at least 60cm (2ft) of space between each, with 75cm (2ft 6in) between rows. Plant them 7.5cm (3in) below the soil surface, then leave well alone until cutting begins in the third year.

Asparagus does best on lighter alluvial soil. If you have heavy soil that retains water, build a gentle mound (about 30cm/1ft high) to aid drainage, planting the crowns at the top of the mound.

SECRETS OF SUCCESS

• See page 95.

> **Did you know?** Asparagus is almost certainly a plant from coastal regions of the Mediterranean and it thrives in light alluvial soils that warm up quickly in spring. Despite that, its range in the wild correlates to the old Roman Empire, indicating that the Romans planted asparagus as a staple, along with vines.

Organic Tip ✔

If planning to plant asparagus, weed the bed very thoroughly in the months before, removing all pernicious weeds. Being weed-free is essential for these shallow-rooted plants.

VARIETIES

For varieties, see June, page 96.

2 Make Leaf Mould
(mid-October)

THE ONE thing October has in abundance is leaves: one minute they cling to the branches, displaying their warm autumnal livery, and the next (usually after a gale-torn night) they are on the ground. Leaves are the source of a magical ingredient called leaf mould and this dark, friable mixture is adored by all plants whether spread as a mulch, added as a soil conditioner or used in potting up.

However, leaves can take up to 2 years to rot down thoroughly, so they cannot be added in huge quantities to a compost heap, although you can get away with small amounts. If space isn't an issue, build yourself a wire frame using chicken netting, then layer in the leaves and allow them to decay. Your dedicated leaf heap may take 18 months to deliver crumbly leaf mould, so you may have to bury next year's leaves underneath.

The leaves have to be damp when you collect them because dry leaves don't rot down. Certain species are slower at producing leaf litter: these include hazel, beech, oak and hornbeam. Others, like sycamore, horse chestnut and lime, are much quicker. Mowing over leaves first chops them up and then they rot down faster.

Many insects, amphibians and small mammals may be hibernating in the warm leafy layer under hedges and shrubs, so let these leaves remain *in situ*.

Did you know? Leaves rot down slowly with the help of fungi; the bacteria found in compost heaps do not do the job. These fungi prefer cooler conditions, so site your wire frame (or store your bags) in a cool position. Well-rotted leaf mould makes a good medium for sowing seeds.

Organic Tip ✔

You can make leaf mould using black plastic dustbin sacks. Collect the leaves and keep some air in the bag, then gently puncture the sides so that air can aid the decomposition process. Store the bags for at least 18 months, then tip the contents out and use the brown crumbly mixture in the same way. The mixture is wetter than leaf mould made in a bin, but still highly useful.

- Avoid evergreen leaves: they are too leathery to rot down.
- Pick up only leaves that are creating a nuisance – e.g. on paths, paving and grass, and on vegetable beds. Leave them to lie on flowerbeds and in quiet corners of the garden so that they rot down *in situ* and provide a habitat for small mammals and insects.
- Leaves on lawns can be chopped up and collected with a mower.
- Use a rubber rake and pick up the leaves by hand, using two small, light pieces of plywood to help.
- Water the leaves if they are dry.
- Transfer the leaves to your wire bin or black bags with your bare hands in case any hedgehogs, toads or frogs are hiding. Put anything back you find, choosing a quiet corner. Thick gardening gloves are too insensitive to allow you to feel hibernating animals. Take them off!

3 Remove Bean Canes
(late October)

IF YOU still have your bean canes in the ground, it's time to get them up and store them away from the wintry weather. Carefully cut any twine that might be binding the canes together and remove any vestige of climbing stems, etc. Using gloves, pull the canes out of the soil and lay them down on the ground. Always handle canes carefully. A bamboo splinter in the hand nearly always goes sceptic and great care has to be taken not to damage the eyes. Goggles would not go amiss.

Go through the canes carefully, separating out any with

broken bottoms, etc. Shorten these with secateurs and store them for other uses. Keep all the long canes and tie them in bundles of ten, making a note of how many replacements you need to buy. An old chimneypot makes a good storage container. Replace some long canes every year, either buying them now or in January. They sell out really quickly in spring and there are never any on offer in May – when you really need them.

Examine any pods. You may have some viable seeds and many gardeners do save their runner bean seeds from year to year. Bring them inside for a day or two to dry, then bag and label them before storing them in an airtight container in a cool place. The seeds are toxic, so do not leave them where children can get hold of them. If you are serious about saving seeds, elect to grow only one variety to lessen the chance of hybridization.

Organic Tip ✔

Bean seeds are viable for an average of 3 years once dried. The seeds are toxic if eaten raw, so always cook them thoroughly before eating them.

SECRETS OF SUCCESS WITH SEED-SAVING

- If saving seeds for a seed crop of any plant visited by bees, stick to one variety or separate them from other similar plants by a 700m (800yd) gap.
- Runner bean varieties often have distinctive seeds, so discard any that differ from the majority.
- Green pods containing seeds can be dried in one piece before de-podding the seeds. However, if you remove seeds that are not fully ripe they will shrivel up and lose viability.

> **Did you know?** Runner beans twist the 'other' way from most beans, climbing clockwise up the canes. Nearly all other beans turn the opposite way. They are also hypogeal: the cotyledons (the embryonic first leaves of the seedling) remain underground while the stem and true leaves emerge.

4 Begin Winter Digging
(late October)

WINTER digging sounds very onerous – but it isn't. All the gardener does is turn over the earth roughly with a fork. It can be done in any weather as long as you stand on a wooden plank to do it. This prevents the soil becoming compacted under your body weight. Two planks are better than one: then you can shuffle between them, moving one whilst standing on the other. Turn in any annual weeds: they will act as a green manure. However, remove any pernicious perennial weeds and any weeds with a seed head. These should be binned – don't compost them. Gardeners with heavier soil should turn it as early as possible because this is the most difficult soil for the weather to break up.

Using a large fork, up-end the soil once and it should form large clods. Resist the urge to break up the clods yourself. Leave them on the ground and their presence will increase the surface area of your soil. When frost occurs, the moisture in the soil will freeze and thaw, breaking up the lumps for you over 3 months or so. By the time spring arrives all you will need to do is rake through the soil and weed it. You will be left with a fine tilth, the perfect fine medium for sowing and planting. Jack Frost is an excellent ally.

Always leave the soil to settle after any digging, weeding or hoeing before you sow and plant, otherwise your seeds could be left on a ridge rather than on a plateau.

Did you know? Medieval gardeners left the weeds in place and ate the edible ones whilst they waited for their crops to mature. They also broadcast-sowed (sprinkled by hand) mixtures of three different crops, which meant that if one failed they still had food. These seed recipes were closely guarded secrets in the time of the Tudor market gardeners who fed London. Sowing single crops in rows did not become popular with gardeners until the mid-nineteenth century when the seed drill began to be used on farms, although Jethro Tull invented a simple seed drill as early as 1701.

Organic Tip ✔

Insect pests identify plants through receptors in their feet and they have to land on the same plant on four consecutive occasions before laying their eggs on it. Mixing up the leaves (as the Tudor gardeners did by sowing three crops together) must have made it harder for pests to target plants.

Insects also home in on the colour green and ignore brown, so a row of plants on the bare earth is an easy target. They don't identify the plant by smell. Scientists at HRI Warwick (Collier and Finch) proved that insects land on green paper as often as they do on green foliage, so the idea that aromatic foliage deters pests is almost certainly incorrect. However, they are confused by mixed plantings when several leaves mingle together.

SECRETS OF SUCCESS FOR SOWING

- When sowing seeds always use a line of string or twine to get straight rows. This saves space and makes it much easier to run the hoe up and down. Two lines are essential for accurate spacing. It's also useful to mark a 60cm (2ft) stick with measurements in centimetres, or inches and feet, which you can use to ensure your lines are parallel.

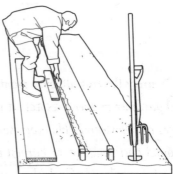

- Make a drill with a trowel or a rake handle. Water it if it's dry or if you are sowing papery seeds like parsnips.
- Sow thinly by tipping the seeds into the palm of your hand and then rubbing them through the fingers.
- Wide drills (about 10cm/4in in width) are excellent for crops like beetroot, parsnips and carrots because they save having to thin out the plants.
- Once the seeds are in the drill, the technique of 'shuffling in' is a useful one. Put one foot on either side of the drill and shuffle along the soil, making small movements. Don't pick your feet up. This will fill in the drill and firm the soil lightly.
- Cover newly sown seeds with chicken wire.
- Thinning plants (if needed) should be done in damp weather, as the seedlings pull out more easily. Cover up any resulting gaps with soil and then water the row again straight after thinning.

NOVEMBER

*S*urely the most gloomy month of all and the one sent to try the gardener in every respect. It is usually drab and damp and the days are shortening. However, sometimes it is mild enough to dig the ground over roughly, or harvest winter crops, or spread manure, or maintain or build. Grab these opportunities. If the weather allows you to get on the ground, don't dally – get on with it. Being pro-active now will save time next spring when there's always too much to do. Charge up your batteries when the weather's against you and plan ahead for next year.

1 Sow 'Aquadulce Claudia' Broad Beans

(*early November*)

THE FIRST week of November is the traditional time to sow the hardiest varieties of broad beans (and early peas) straight into the ground. The seeds should start to germinate within 2 or 3 weeks, although in cold winters they may not appear above the ground until the New Year. Cover the rows to prevent mice and birds from eating the seeds and young plants. Chicken wire is usually adequate, although some gardeners resort to mousetraps in order to protect their peas and beans.

November sowings of both are a gamble. Seeds always do best in cold winters rather than warm, wet ones that stop and start. Sometimes the seeds fail to germinate in wet winters and rot in the ground. The young plants and emerging seeds can be eaten by mice, rats and pigeons and an autumn-sown crop will give you broad beans only 3 weeks earlier than early-spring sowings. Yet those 3 weeks are important because this crop can deliver in June when little else is available. November-sown crops grow slowly, but their root systems are strong and deep and generally the crop is heavy.

> **Did you know?** Green mustard sprays, garlic washes, soft soap and dilute washing-up liquid sound a lot friendlier than insecticides and they may not linger in the environment like a branded chemical. However, they wreak just as much havoc in your ecosystem because they kill predators and pests indiscriminately. Remember your breeding birds need those insects, and if you feel a problem is getting away from you, attack the aphids or other pests with your fingers.

SECRETS OF SUCCESS

- You are in the lap of the gods at this time of year. For this reason, sow plenty of seeds and always cover them with wire. Remember the old adage: 'One for the mouse, One for the crow, One to rot and one to grow.'
- Zig-zag peas thickly across a 22cm (9in) wide trench. Add the wire and then the twiggy stakes immediately.
- Broad beans can be sown by dropping in one seed per hole to a depth of 5cm (2in) with 20cm (8in) spacings between them. Each pair of double rows should be 60cm (24in) apart. Sow a handful of seeds at each end of the row for gapping up any seeds that fail.
- If the November crop fails, send up a prayer and re-sow in late January. This is also the time to plug any gaps.

VARIETIES OF BROAD BEAN AND PEA

**Broad Bean
'Aquadulce Claudia' AGM**
The classic broad bean for November and early-spring sowing. This compact variety (90cm/3ft) produces large white beans.

**Pea
'Douce de Provence'**
Another round-seeded pea that can be sown in early November.

**Pea
'Feltham First'**
Round-seeded, dwarf variety (45cm/18in) for autumn sowing. Good cold tolerance. Pointed, straight pod 8cm (3½in) long, with seven or eight peas per pod. This hardy pea overwinters consistently well and crops heavily.

2 Make a Rotation Plan
(early November)

ROTATION plans involve growing crops in different places every
year and are vital to all gardeners because they help improve yields.
Crops exhaust the soil in different ways, so moving them on helps
them to find the nutrients they need in fresher soil. Rotation also
prevents a build-up of pests and diseases, especially soil-borne
ones. If carrot root flies have been a problem, for instance, they
should fade away if there are no carrots to feed on for 4 years.

Rotation plans can be incredibly complex, but I believe the
simplest method is the best. A 4-year rotation works well. Divide
your crops into the following categories – potatoes, legumes (i.e.,
peas and beans), brassicas and roots – and keep them in that order.
The theory behind this is that potatoes exhaust the soil. The
legumes replace the nitrogen used by the potatoes and this then
feeds the brassicas that will follow on. Roots (and onions) come last
and then every fourth year the plot is manured over winter.
Confusingly, some root-forming crops are brassicas, including
turnips, swedes and kohl rabi. These are subject to the same pests
and diseases as other brassicas, so include them in the brassica
section and not with the roots.

A 4-year rotation needs four equal-sized pieces of ground.

However, any practical gardener will know that the theory of sticking to a rotation plan is difficult, because you will squeeze crops that fall between the groups into gaps. These include sweetcorn and all cucurbits (squashes, courgettes, cucumbers, etc.). It is a yearly balancing act.

The important crops to move every year are potatoes, as they suffer from blight, eel-worm and scab. Root crops are prone to root fly and canker and they too should be strictly rotated.

SECRETS OF SUCCESS

- Make sure that every fourth year the ground is thoroughly enriched with well-rotted organic matter, either animal manure or material from your compost heap. This will improve soil structure and nutrients, and your soil will not dry out as readily.
- Use easy-to-apply sprinkle-on, organic fertilizers and liquid feeds to boost nutrients as appropriate and as recommended by the maker. Remember that these boost nutrients for a while but do not improve soil structure (see Fertilizers overleaf).
- Over-feeding soil results in soft, sappy growth that is prone to disease and insect attack.
- Remove all self-set potatoes as soon as they appear, as they could harbour disease and pests. They will also disrupt your pea and bean crops.
- Analyse problems and act accordingly. If potatoes continually get scab, look for a scab-resistant variety.
- Always select excellent varieties, preferably those with an award of Garden Merit (AGM).

Did you know? Vegetable rotation was widely practised in
Britain until the mid-nineteenth century when spread-on
fertilizers became the fashion. Guano, the nitrogen-rich
droppings of anchovy-fed sea birds collected from the
coast of Peru, saw the rotation system's demise. Previously
this odourless material had been used by the Incas. The
first shipment arrived in Britain in 1842 and it soon
became the country's most popular fertilizer, making
fortunes for entrepreneurs like William Gibbs, who built
Tyntesfield House near Nailsea, Bristol, for £70,000 –
one year's profits.

THE EASIEST FERTILIZERS

Blood, Fish and Bone
An all-purpose, well-balanced, slow-release plant food for building fertility.
Can be used when planting or sprinkled on later. Easy to handle and good for brassicas.

Bonemeal
A slow-acting source of phosphorus with nitrogen, best for developing good root systems.

Chicken Manure Pellets
Nitrogen-rich and easy to apply, but the smell can put gardeners off and attract the interest of foxes. Dogs will also consume the pellets. There are powdered forms too.

3 Plant a Native Hedge
(late November)

HEDGES are extremely useful to the vegetable gardener because they provide shelter from the wind and encourage and sustain birdlife. The end of November is an excellent time to plant bare-root whips to make a hedge. These arrive between now and early March looking rather like long sticks. They are inexpensive to buy (and post) and establish themselves quickly, as long as they don't have to struggle with weeds.

Native hedges contain species that have adapted to our conditions. They produce fruit and flowers that suit our wildlife, so they attract much more insect life than non-natives. These insects are vital to breeding birds – and birds are extremely good predators, so it's important to sustain them.

> **Did you know?** Our native hawthorn (*Crataegus monogyna*) is the most appealing hedge of all to insects and can attract up to 149 species. The horse chestnut (*Aesculus hippocastanum*), which is an alien species, will attract only fifteen. So it makes good sense to plant a native hedge.

Organic Tip ✔

Source your hedging whips from a reputable supplier to ensure your hedge will flower and come into leaf at the correct time. Ask your supplier for information, as some hedging material grown in eastern Europe is not suitable in the UK. It may be the right species but the wrong ecotype: e.g., blackthorn from eastern European stock flowers far too early here to be of any benefit to our predators.

SECRETS OF SUCCESS

- Prepare the soil well before planting – preferably in the autumn. Dig a trench 45cm (18in) wide and 30cm (1ft) deep along the length of the proposed hedge. Improve the ground if you can by adding generous amounts of garden compost or well-rotted manure. If your soil is poorly drained, add sharp sand or coarse grit.
- If you want a thicker hedge, plant a double row about 60cm (2ft) apart.
- When the plants arrive, unwrap them and soak them for up to 2 hours in water. If the ground is frozen or waterlogged, before the plants arrive prepare a 'back-up' slit trench about 50cm (20in) deep in a sheltered place to rest your plants for safety before planting. Cover the trench with old carpet or polythene to keep the ground frost-free.
- Once planted, mulch well with at least 5–10cm (2–4in) of bark chips or other mulching material. This will suppress weed growth and retain moisture.
- Keep the young hedge well watered during its first growing season. In windy sites you may need to use windbreak netting.
- Leave the hedge bottom undisturbed, particularly in winter. The leaf litter will shelter amphibians, spiders, beetles, small mammals and insects. You may well have hibernating toads, hedgehogs and voles under your hedge.
- Cut your hedge in late winter. The best shape is an A, with the widest part of the hedge being at the base. This shape provides more shelter and the sides of the hedge get more sunlight.

VARIETIES OF NATIVE HEDGING

Hawthorn/Quickthorn (*Crataegus monogyna*)
Fast-growing, spiny deciduous plant tolerant of wet soils. Dark, glossy green leaves, clusters of prominent, scented white flowers in May followed by plentiful red haws in autumn. Very hardy and useful in coastal or exposed positions.

Blackthorn or Sloe (*Prunus spinosa*)
A dense, prickly deciduous plant. New shoots have a fine down but become smooth by winter, and are purple in sun or green in shade. Masses of snow-white flowers appear in March before the leaves, and these are followed by sloes, which turn from purple to black in autumn. Any soil, but will thrive on quite poor soil.

Dogwood (*Cornus sanguinea*)
A deciduous shrub with green stems flushed with red. Rich, damson-red autumn colouring. Any soil, very chalk-tolerant and thrives in a very damp position.

Spindle (*Euonymus europaeus*)
Green-stemmed deciduous shrub with inconspicuous flowers in May. Good autumn colour and the red and orange spindles attract birds, particularly robins. Spindle is a host plant for beet and bean aphids – so this is one you may want to avoid. Any ordinary soil, sun or partial shade.

Dog Rose (*Rosa canina*)
Arching branches bearing white to pale-pink, single flowers in June, followed by glossy red hips in autumn. Loved by birds in winter.

Hazel (*Corylus avellana*)
Deciduous shrub with large, mid-green leaves that appear with the bluebells. Long, yellow catkins in early spring are followed by edible nuts in autumn. Cut in winter for stakes and poles.

4 Set Up Water Butts
(late November)

IN THE days of the old walled kitchen garden there was always a dipping pond in the heart of the garden where you could go to fill up the watering can with rainwater. This precious liquid was at just the right temperature for the plants. Tapwater, which tends to be heavy on chlorine, is not nearly as good for mature plants as rainwater.

November, when there's less to do in the garden, is the

perfect month to think about capturing some of that precious precipitation. Sadly, most of us have to catch our rainwater in a water butt positioned close to a shed or greenhouse. Most are not very exciting to look at, although you can order Grecian urn shapes and wooden barrels. Go for the largest you can comfortably site and make sure that it has a lid. This will prevent any accidents with children, small animals and birds. It will also stop mosquito larvae breeding.

Gardeners should not be using mains/drinking water for watering, except for seedlings. It is in short supply in many parts of the country and in years to come new-build houses will almost certainly be fitted with rainwater- and grey-water-harvesting systems as a compulsory feature.

Did you know? It was illegal to collect rainwater in the US state of Colorado until 2009. However, new research carried out in 2007 found that 97 per cent of the precipitation that fell in Douglas County in Denver never reached a stream. It was used by plants or evaporated on the ground. As a result of this finding, the ban on collecting rainwater was lifted.

SECRETS OF SUCCESS

- Make sure the tap on your butt is high enough to get a full-sized can underneath. Most water butts have a stand that supports them safely.
- If you live in a very dry area, invest in a square or rectangular tank. It will hold much more water.
- Order your tank from someone who can deliver it – they are not car-friendly items!

Organic Tip ✔

If 2.5cm (1in) of rain falls on 1,000 square feet of roof, it will yield 623 gallons of water. That would fill over 300 watering cans.

DECEMBER

*T*he days are at their shortest now, but winter vegetables should be in good supply and leeks, parsnips, kale and Brussels sprouts help make winter bearable in the run-up to the shortest day.

Whenever the weather is clement, get outside and dig over any un-dug ground roughly – provided it is dry enough. If it's too damp underfoot, titivate and trim the edges and take out any weeds. Stand on a board if you have to. The really cold weather is more likely to bite in the New Year, but by then the days will be drawing out and that's a comforting thought for every gardener.

1 Clean Your Tools
(early December)

IDEALLY your garden tools should be cleaned after every use, but reality falls short of this expectation for most of us. My homage to daily cleaning is plunging the blades of my spade and fork into the bucket of damp sharp sand by my shed door. As long as the sand is damp it will keep the blade clean and sharp. Hand trowels and forks get the bucket-plunging treatment too.

But now it is worth having a blitz on everything in the shed, from rakes to brooms to shears. Arm yourself with newspaper and old cloths, buy some linseed oil and get busy. Wipe all wooden handles with a damp cloth and dry them before oiling the handles liberally. If the wood feels too rough, sand it off beforehand. An oily cloth can also be wiped over the metal to prevent rust. Store your tools off the ground, placing rakes and brooms head up. Check the wheelbarrow too.

This yearly clean makes it a joy to handle tools the following year. Most of us are devoted to our favourite fork or spade and keeping it in fine fettle is important. However, if replacements are needed this is an excellent time of the year to break new ones in, because you have more time to get used to them.

Tools make excellent Christmas presents. I particularly admire stainless-steel spades, but I always handle a garden tool to make sure the whole thing feels balanced before buying or dropping a strong hint for Christmas. Good secateurs are essential too, though very expensive. A good pair should last a lifetime.

If you have a mower that needs servicing, get it sorted out now before spring arrives.

> **Did you know?** The wheelbarrow is believed to have been invented by the Chinese general Chuko Liang (AD 181–234), who used wooden wheelbarrows to transport supplies and collect injured soldiers. His wheelbarrow had two wheels and required two men to propel and steer it. The earliest evidence of a European (or single-wheeled) wheelbarrow is found in a stained-glass window in Chartres Cathedral in France and dates from 1220. The wheel is near the front to provide enough leverage for move heavy loads.

Organic Tip ✔

Be sustainable where possible and use oak labels, metal cans and jute string. They might cost more, but the joy of having materials that blend into the garden is worth the extra cost.

2 Tame the Snail
(early December)

ONE OF the most valuable things you can do now is go on a snail hunt for hibernating clusters. You'll find them against sheltered walls and behind plants. Having sealed up their shells, they hug together in clusters that can be as large as a football. If you can locate them now, before they wake up in spring, you can save yourself a lot of trouble. Check under water butts, close to sheds, in the greenhouse and in any sheltered nooks and crannies.

Snails are not slimy to handle at the moment and if you crush them hungry thrushes and blackbirds can reap the benefits. Once spring and summer arrive, snails will be on the move throughout the day. Lay small plastic pots on their sides and check them daily for sheltering snails. They also like to slide up and down linear leaves, so you often find them on irises, pokers and hemerocallis. Learn to frisk susceptible plants regularly – wear rubber gloves if you're squeamish.

If you squash some snails on the path as dark falls in spring and summer, I can guarantee that slugs will appear to devour their remains. Slugs are creatures of the night, coming out as darkness falls to seek prey. That's the best time to hunt them down.

Did you know? The common garden snail (*Helix aspersa*) is the fastest species of snail. It can move about 55 m (60yd) per hour. They are also very strong – they can lift ten times their own body weight. They hate bright sunlight. Snails sniff out their food despite the fact that their two upper tentacles have eye-like light sensors. The shorter two are for feeling.

Organic Tip ✔

The song thrush relies on the snail as a staple food and one brood of thrushes will eat hundreds. The latest research suggests that they eat snails when the ground has become baked or frozen and they cannot dig out worms. The bird will smash the snail's shell against a stone, so having some flat pieces of rock in your garden is a great help to them.

3 Sort and Order Vegetable Seeds

(mid–late December)

TIME TO sort out your old packets of seeds and decide what to buy for next year. Seeds that have a really short viability are parsnips (2 years), carrots (3 years) and sweetcorn (2 years). Check the dates of these carefully. Many seeds (including runner beans, beetroot, cabbages and lettuce) can store for 5 years in perfect conditions. However, open packets can deteriorate and I find lettuce seeds have a tendency to do so.

When ordering, it's often worth investing in F1 vegetable seeds, although they are expensive and you always get fewer seeds. However, they have hybrid vigour and produce a crop enthusiastically. Their seeds also germinate more readily, so F1 varieties of sweetcorn and parsnip (both troublesome in their own way) are well worth the investment, as is F1 spinach.

In recent years vegetable-breeders have risen to the organic challenge by breeding disease-resistant varieties, so seek these out. Look out for eastern European varieties too: these are often very hardy, prolific and disease-resistant because chemicals were not widely used in eastern Europe, as they were too costly.

There has also been a breakthrough in bean-breeding and there are new French × runner bean crosses. The first was 'Moonlight', a bean that looks like a cream-flowered runner. The French bean blood allows it to crop for longer (even in hot weather) and the individual beans are plumper – see page 74.

Balance the expense of F1 varieties by ordering well-established, top-performing AGM varieties like pea 'Hurst Greenshaft' and broad bean 'Jubilee Hysor'. Thompson & Morgan have an AGM section. If you have a variety that works for you, stick to it.

4 Force Witloof Chicory

(mid–late December)

WITLOOF chicory is a very useful crop because you can lift the roots from late November onwards and force a few roots at a time. This provides a vegetable during winter when the ground may be frozen or even covered in snow. The crunchy, pale leaves are good either cooked as a vegetable or eaten raw in a salad – a reminder of summer past.

Lift four or five roots and use scissors or shears to cut off the tops to within 2.5cm (1in) of the top of the rootstock. Place them in a large pot full of compost so that the tops are proud of the soil. Cover them with a bucket so that they are in the dark, then leave them in a cool place (average temperature 16–18°C (61–64°F) for 3–4 weeks. In that time a pointed sheath of crispy, pale leaves will appear: this is known as a chicon. You can slow the process down by moving the pots outside if you wish.

You can force other chicories and endives, or you can use them for leaf. However, the seeds are sown at different times. Cultivars of chicory (*Cichorium intybus*) for forcing are sown in May and June. Leafy varieties are sown a month later, in June and July. Endive (*Cichorium endivia*) can be sown from April to August. Sow thinly to a depth of 0.5cm (½in) in rows 30cm (12in) apart.

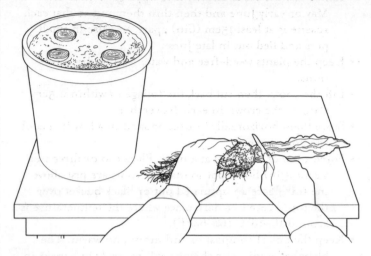

Did you know? After the discovery of blanched chicory in Belgium in 1830 (see page 78), a horticulturist from Brussels Botanical Garden refined the forcing process and chicons were first sold in Brussels market in 1846. However, forced chicory did not become widely eaten until the 1920s and 1930s.

Organic Tip ✔

Don't sow the seeds for forcing too early in the year, otherwise your plants could bolt. Thin the seedlings carefully so that they form large roots and then you will produce large chicons.

SECRETS OF SUCCESS

- Either sow the seeds directly into open ground in late May or early June and then thin them out so that each rosette is at least 15cm (6in) apart, or raise in small pots and bed out in late June.
- Keep the plants weed-free and water well in dry conditions.
- Lift the roots, then cut back the foliage to within 2.5cm (1in) of the crown in early November.
- Store them horizontally in peat or sand in a box in a cool shed or garage.
- Force a few of the roots at a time. Place two or three in a 22cm (9in) flowerpot so that the roots are just above the soil. Place an upturned pot or black bucket over the top. Leave in a dark place where the temperature is around 16–18°C (61–64°F).
- Keep the pot of compost or soil moist and warm. The blanched endives or chicons will be ready to harvest in about 3–4 weeks.
- When harvesting a chicon, cut into the rootstock or the chicon will fall apart.

VARIETIES

For other varieties of chicory, see May, page 77.

INDEX

INDEX

NOTES

Val Bourne has been a fanatical gardener since the age of five. In her twenties she worked in vegetable research, at a lowly level, and she has always grown her own fruit and vegetables organically. She now has a large allotment, and fruit and vegetable patches amongst her extensive flower garden in the Cotswolds.

An award-winning writer, Val also serves on two RHS panels – dahlias and herbaceous and tender plants, which meet fortnightly to assess plants for the Award of Garden Merit (AGM). She lectures all over the UK and has also lectured in Japan and South Africa. Val writes regularly for the *Daily Telegraph*, *Saga* magazine, *Oxford Times*, *Grow It* and the Hardy Plant Society magazine. She also contributes to the RHS *The Garden*, and *The Rose Magazine*, amongst other publications.

She is the author of six other books, including *The Natural Gardener* (winner of the Gardening Writers' Guild Practical Book of the Year), *The Winter Garden*, *Colour in the Garden* and *Seeds of Wisdom*, as well as *The Ten-Minute Gardener's Fruit-Growing Diary* and *The Ten-Minute Gardener's Flower-Growing Diary*.

Her passion is still gardening!